MAKING DREAMS COME TRUE

MAKING DREAMS COME TRUE

THE STORY OF THE TECH MAHINDRA FOUNDATION

VINOD C. KHANNA

PORTFOLIO
PENGUIN

PORTFOLIO
Published by the Penguin Group
Penguin Books India Pvt. Ltd, 7th Floor, Infinity Tower C, DLF Cyber City, Gurgaon 122 002, Haryana, India
Penguin Group (USA) Inc., 375 Hudson Street, New York, New York 10014, USA
Penguin Group (Canada), 90 Eglinton Avenue East, Suite 700, Toronto, Ontario, M4P 2Y3, Canada
Penguin Books Ltd, 80 Strand, London WC2R 0RL, England
Penguin Ireland, 25 St Stephen's Green, Dublin 2, Ireland
(a division of Penguin Books Ltd)
Penguin Group (Australia), 707 Collins Street, Melbourne, Victoria 3008, Australia
Penguin Group (NZ), 67 Apollo Drive, Rosedale, Auckland 0632, New Zealand
Penguin Books (South Africa) (Pty) Ltd, Block D, Rosebank Office Park, 181 Jan Smuts Avenue, Parktown North, Johannesburg 2193, South Africa

Penguin Books Ltd, Registered Offices: 80 Strand, London WC2R 0RL, England

First published in Portfolio by Penguin Books India 2014

10 9 8 7 6 5 4 3 2 1

ISBN 9780670087631

Typeset in Adobe Garamond Pro by Eleven Arts, Delhi
Printed at Replika Press Pvt. Ltd, India

A PENGUIN RANDOM HOUSE COMPANY

Gandhiji's talisman

I will give you a talisman. Whenever you are in doubt, or when the self becomes too much with you, apply the following test. Recall the face of the poorest and the weakest man whom you may have seen, and ask yourself if the step you contemplate is going to be of any use to him. Will he gain anything by it? Will it restore him to a control over his own life and destiny?

Board of Directors

'At the Mahindra Group, Corporate Social Responsibility is not just a duty; it's a way of life.'

Keshub Mahindra, Chairman Emeritus, Mahindra & Mahindra
Chairman, Board of Directors, Tech Mahindra Foundation

'Mankind would be in a dangerous state if people were not sensitive to the pain of others. I would not like to be such an individual nor part of a group or company which was not sensitive to the pain and need of others.'
Anand Mahindra, Chairman and Managing Director, Mahindra & Mahindra
Director, Tech Mahindra Foundation

'We have been doing splendid work through the Tech Mahindra Foundation and continue to do so. But is that enough? I firmly believe that true Corporate Social Responsibility in a corporate goes far beyond the signing of the cheque. I believe it comes with every individual in the organization believing in the cause we support. It comes with each one of us complementing and contributing to the cause. It comes with all of us unanimously wanting to make a difference to that cause.'

Vineet Nayyar, Executive Vice Chairman, Tech Mahindra
Director, Tech Mahindra Foundation

Contents

Preface

Business has long recognized the power and influence it wields and has, in many instances, used this for the betterment of the environment it inhabits or the communities it interacts with. The Tatas, Birlas, Singhanias are all great examples of this.

However, such activities have traditionally been seen as philanthropy, or giving back—a feel-good gesture, rather than an intrinsic part of doing business. I believe the time has come for a shift in paradigm. There is an outcry across the world for businesses to be more alive to issues larger than their profits, especially after the Big-Bad-Wolf image that businesses have earned during the recession. Today, there is a lack of credibility and trust between society and business. This glaring gap is not good for business, or for society, and companies that cannot overcome it will quickly erode their brand, and lose the trust of the public. Hence, businesses must build the creation of shared value into their business strategy. Creating shared value for all stakeholders, including the wider community, has now become an essential part of doing business and is what will distinguish the successful business of the twenty-first century from the unsuccessful one. In other words, the age of the purpose-driven organization has come.

India, with its extremes of aspiration and deprivation, is a fertile playing field for those who believe in this philosophy.

Tech Mahindra is definitely a purpose-driven organization and has been invested in the communities in which it operates for many years now.

In his *Nitishatakam*, the sixth century Sanskrit poet Bhartrihari lauds those who give secretly and maintain silence in public about their good deeds. Tech Mahindra Foundation (TMF) has generally followed the Bhartrihari dictum and has exercised modest reserve regarding its work. However, at this point in our nation's development, I believe there is great value to be derived from sharing the story of how a medium-sized private Foundation can contribute to some of our country's important developmental goals and bring about a transformation for the better in the lives of thousands of disadvantaged young people. It is the story of how a business can do well and do good at the same time, and help people everywhere to rise.

Vinod C. Khanna, the author, led TMF for several years prior to his recent retirement and has great expertise in the developmental field. He tells the TMF story in a down to earth and factual way, sharing learnings as well as achievements. I hope this book will be an inspiration and a road map for those who believe that profits and social good can and must go hand in hand and that creating shared value is the road to future business success.

Anand G. Mahindra

1

Introduction

Tech Mahindra, like all other members of the Mahindra group, and indeed like any good company, is deeply conscious of its responsibility to the society at large. A primary instrument for performing its Corporate Social Responsibility (CSR) is the Tech Mahindra Foundation (TMF). TMF is an important instrument of Tech Mahindra's CSR but not the sole one. Tech Mahindra is very mindful of its other social responsibilities as well, such as ethical functioning, respect for the rights and welfare of its workers and respect for the environment.

One of Tech Mahindra's main offices: Hinjewadi, Pune

TMF's work is not related to the commercial interests of the company Tech Mahindra. Of course, any firm's reputation for philanthropy does help in enhancing its image, making it more attractive as a business partner. But that is a welcome spin-off rather than the Foundation's defining mission.

TMF was registered as a Section 25 company under the Companies Act on 22 March 2006, less than two months after Mahindra-British Telecom was converted into Tech Mahindra. But 2007 marked a major milestone in the history of the Foundation. A new board of directors—with Keshub Mahindra as chairman and Anand Mahindra and Vineet Nayyar as members—took over the leadership of the Foundation. The fact that the chairman and vice chairman of the entire Mahindra group and the CEO of the company were leading the Foundation announced to the world the priority and importance assigned to this major instrument of Tech Mahindra's corporate responsibility. I was asked to head the executive team.

The new board met for the first time on 19 April 2007 and addressed such fundamental issues as the objectives of the Foundation and its strategy for achieving them. The board was conscious, right at the outset, of the need to have a well-defined focus, lest the resources of the Foundation be frittered away chasing too many goals. There is, after all, no dearth of deserving causes in our country. After due deliberation, the board decided that the primary objective would be education of the underprivileged children and youth. Education would be broadly defined to also include vocational training of economically challenged youth so as to help them become self-reliant. There would be special focus on the vulnerable: the girl child, physically challenged and minorities.

> 'Education is the most powerful weapon which you can use to change the world.'
> Nelson Mandela

The decision to concentrate primarily on education was because the Foundation regards it as the most effective instrument for empowerment of an individual—though it is, of course, not sufficient by itself. Further, it is obvious that education is the critical input for the kind of human resources that help propel a society forward.

Along with prioritizing women's empowerment through education, TMF believes that if India is to be a fair, just and prosperous society, it is important that all members of its multi-religious, multilingual and multicultural population advance together.

The board also agreed that TMF would work primarily through good NGOs; to begin with, it would concentrate its work in and around Pune, Mumbai, Delhi–Noida and Bangalore.

When Tech Mahindra bought over Satyam in 2009, I was entrusted with the responsibility of running the Hyderabad-based Mahindra Satyam Foundation as well.

In April 2012, the Mahindra Satyam Foundation formally merged with the Tech Mahindra Foundation, which now became a significantly bigger organization both in terms of the funds at its disposal and the size of its staff. Shortly before that, I retired from the Foundation after having served for five years, and Dr Loveleen Kacker, a Madhya Pradesh cadre IAS officer, who had just retired from the government, took over as CEO. With the growing profits of Tech Mahindra, the Foundation she leads has expanded greatly. The writing of this book was basically finished by the end of the year 2013. Major developments would, no doubt, continue to take place under her leadership.

The journey of the Tech Mahindra Foundation from 2007 to the present has been marked by a constant process of self-evaluation, refinement and new endeavours with continuous advice from the operations committee led by Vineet Nayyar and the overall guidance of the board of directors. Basing itself on the clear cut objectives outlined by the board, TMF has been able to make a modest contribution to sustainable improvement in the lives of thousands of economically, socially or physically disadvantaged children and young persons.

2

Our Modus Operandi

The Tech Mahindra company is the Foundation's sole source of funding. At the beginning of each year, the Foundation is told about the amount to expect for its work. During most of the period covered by this book, the company donated 1.5 per cent of its profit-after-taxation to the Foundation. As those who have to run development support organizations without such guaranteed funding know only too well, this has been a great asset. We could do our annual planning without any sense of uncertainty about availability and adequacy of funding. Showing great foresight, the board of directors each year sets apart a certain amount towards building a corpus.

Having decided to work primarily in partnership with NGOs, it was important to locate the most appropriate not-for-profit voluntary organizations functioning in our chosen fields and to build an appropriate relationship with them.

We align our grants with the social ideals we believe in. While we do not ourselves undertake campaigns for or against issues/problems, we ensure that we select as partners NGOs whose general philosophy resembles ours, be it secularism, gender equality, inclusive growth or fundamental freedoms.

In the initial stages, it was the Foundation's team that had to undertake a search for good partner NGOs but, gradually, as word spread, many NGOs themselves approached us. In either case, rigorous due diligence was mandatory. It was necessary to assure ourselves that the NGO shared our vision and values, had the necessary skills and was respected in the community it intended to serve.

NGOs have to submit their proposals in a carefully prepared format. This is designed to secure essential background information such as its governance and management structure, legal and financial status and its vision and mission as articulated by the NGO itself. As per this form, the NGO must also provide detailed information on the proposed project, including a situational analysis (socio-economic-cultural aspects) as well as project need-assessment, planned activities, budget and, perhaps most important of all, the expected outcomes, both quantitative and qualitative.

If, prima facie, the proposal appears attractive, we undertake an in-depth discussion with the top leadership of the NGO and field visits to verify the claims made in the proposal. One defining feature of a good NGO working for the poor is that it does not approach them with condescension but empathy and compassion.

The Foundation team then prepares executive summaries of the proposals that merit support in its view. Originally, all proposals for grants to NGOs would come to the board of directors for approval. But as the work expanded, it was decided to constitute an Operations Committee, which throughout this period was chaired by Vineet Nayyar assisted by Milind Kulkarni, CFO of the company. Initially there was a third member, Jayanti Patil, who was Head of Technical Training in the company. But her true passion was CSR and she was a great help as we began our operations in Pune. Unfortunately, because of ill health she had to retire.

At the meetings of the Ops Committee, each new proposal is scrutinized meticulously and the executive team grilled on all aspects. Many a proposal is dropped if it does not meet the high standards set by Vineet and Milind.

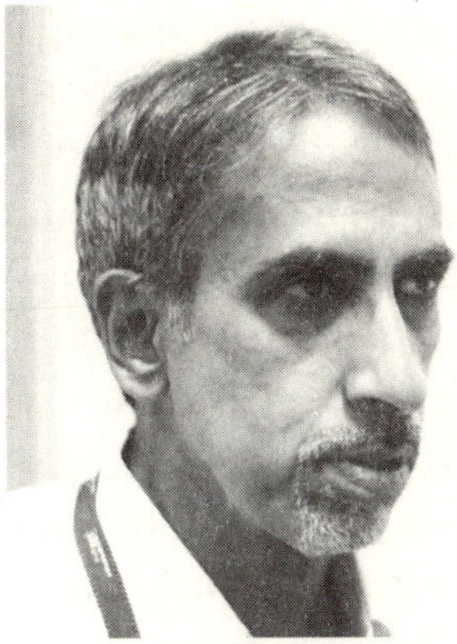

Milind Kulkarni

If the proposal is approved by the Ops Committee, a memorandum of understanding (MoU) is signed between TMF and the concerned NGO. This is based on a template drawn up in consultation with the legal wing of Tech Mahindra. The objective is to ensure a fair and balanced relationship between the two entities, with clearly defined mutual obligations. It states how much money would be given for what purpose and on what terms and conditions. Great care is taken to ensure financial rectitude and accountability.

The MoU also incorporates an agreement by the implementing NGO that the representatives of the Foundation can visit the project from time to time to assess its progress. The mode and periodicity of reporting is laid down.

Of course, even after every care has been exercised in the selection of an NGO partner, things can still go wrong. Hence, there is this clause in the MoU: the Foundation '*reserves the right to vary, amend and / or stop any contribution, in full or any part of it, if the Foundation, at its sole discretion, determines that the programme is not being implemented as per the MoU or that any part of the contribution (a) has not been used or is not likely to be used for the approved purposes or (b) has been misused or misappropriated or (c) is likely to be misused or misappropriated . . .*'

While it is important to have a legal document to underpin an arrangement in which, after all, the Foundation is committing a substantial amount of money, the true value and spirit of the partnership lies in building a relationship of mutual trust. A good partnership between the two does not happen automatically. The worst combination would be a hegemonic donor and a subservient NGO. Some NGOs are so desperately dependent on the donor agency that they adopt an obsequious attitude, surrendering their own goals and judgement to the agenda and demands of the donor. At the other extreme are a few NGOs who expect a blank cheque and are resentful of even well-meaning attempts to engage them in a dialogue about their work. We in TMF have gone out of our way to build a relationship of equality, and to permit them sufficient independence of judgement. Our team did not hesitate to offer advice and guidance when that was necessary. As I often said to my team, take your time in assessing a potential partner—if necessary ask uncomfortable questions—but once they are on board, their success is our success, their failure is our failure.

We were deeply touched when Sheetal Amte, the granddaughter of Baba Amte who now runs Anandwan along with his other descendants, told us about how she had often been discouraged by the attitude of some other funding organizations and contrasted this with the sensitivity shown by the TMF executives. To quote her words, 'A prominent feature of TMF family is here "retardations and failures" have been accepted by my associates of TMF as "evolutionary learning", as against the other funders where failures led to denial of chances to innovate.'

Good performance is a necessary precondition for renewal of partnership. While every consideration is extended to the fact that almost all our partners are dealing with difficult and complex issues, with ever-present dangers of work being adversely impacted by

> 'The biggest strength of this Foundation is that they have listened to us and tried to match our needs rather than giving us what was convenient for them.'
> Dr Sheetal Amte, Secretary, Anandwan

unexpected external factors, a very dim view is taken of any false reporting. Zero–absolutely zero—tolerance is extended to any financial misdemeanour. Of the 100 or so organizations we assisted during this period, only two were found guilty of deliberate cheating.

Often, donor agencies demand an unrealistic level of idealism from NGOs. They sometimes expect all who work in the NGO sector to be Gandhian ascetics who must work on little or preferably no payment. For an NGO to run a programme, it needs administrators, project officers, field staff and accountants. The NGO must pay not fancy corporate salaries but an adequate amount for a decent living if it has to attract and retain quality personnel. (Of course, many come from well-to-do families and may voluntarily opt to work on a purely honorary basis but they would be the exceptions.) To this one must add office expenses such as rent, electricity, communication etc. While refusing to fund extravagance or avoidable waste, our Foundation has been willing to give NGOs the resources they needed to function efficiently.

Another challenge in determining an optimal relationship is the time-frame in which the NGO should show significant results. All those involved in the development field are aware that social change often takes an unpredictably long time. Indeed, the progress is sometimes so slow as to be imperceptible. There are times when despite the NGO's best efforts the hoped for outcomes do not occur. In such cases, there has to be an assessment on whether a little

> TMF supported two of Swadhar's projects during 2008–13. I can still remember the day when I met Mr Khanna in his office to discuss the project proposal for out-of-school children. Our proposal had hesitantly asked for a small figure for teaching aids and material. Mr Khanna told me to double it and advised me not to compromise on essentials. This philosophy was reflected at all times during our partnership. We will always remember and appreciate this approach.
>
> Anjali Bapat, Member, Managing Committee, Swadhar, Pune

more patience would yield desired results or whether it is time for course correction. Of course, if the failure is due to obvious incompetence—or worse, due to deliberate misbehaviour—one has no option but to abandon the NGO.

There had been intensive debate on the duration of the Foundation's support to any particular NGO. Many donor agencies limit their support to three years. The rationale behind this approach is that a NGO should during this period either have completed the project or become self-sufficient or have acquired ability to raise funds from other sources so that the funding agency can move on to other equally deserving organizations. Finally, in 2011 the Ops Committee decided that the Foundation would normally phase out after five years of a partnership. However, the Committee agreed to make several exceptions to this rule. Thus, for instance, organizations serving the visually impaired were not covered under this time limitation nor were those working for the hearing and speech impaired. Further exception was extended to those NGOs with whom the content of the programmes changed significantly. Our account will also include many of those NGOs from which we have phased out under the five-year rule.

Environmentalist Sunita Narain speaking in her capacity as a jury member of the Times of India Social Impact Awards on 28 January 2013 made an interesting point about a dilemma faced by the jury: how does one compare the work of a well-established NGO operating on a large scale with that of a relatively new arrival who perforce has begun small. If you do not support the latter, even if it clearly has the potential to do excellent work, how will it ever become 'well-established'? You cannot expect it to be Minerva-like, born with all perfection. We in TMF have tried for a healthy mix of experienced NGOs with an impressive track record and relatively new ones, assuming of course that the latter display adequate domain knowledge and commitment. Certain amount of risk-taking was inevitable.

Naturally, there has to be continuous objective monitoring by the Foundation for which the fundamental criterion is delivery of what has been promised in the NGO's proposal. Modalities for this were carefully worked out. The experience of other donor agencies was studied as was the literature on the subject.

Once we have taken on a NGO partner, our general assumption has to be that they are people with integrity trying to work in difficult circumstances. We need to give them a reasonable degree of flexibility while ensuring that no money is wasted or goes down a corrupt route. We check their accounts annually as a second line of defence over and above the statutory audit reports which they are mandated to submit. Where big accounts are concerned we request professional auditors to conduct an independent appraisal.

A brief word about the internal functioning of the Foundation.

Even after the constitution of the Ops Committee, the meetings of the board of directors are held to determine the larger policy issues. The broad outlines of the annual plan are submitted to them for approval. The Foundation profits immensely from the vast experience, the razor sharp minds and unfailing pragmatism of Keshub Mahindra, Anand Mahindra and Vineet Nayyar. New ideas are discussed intensely in an atmosphere marked by profound concern for the underprivileged. It then becomes the responsibility of the executive team to convert these ideas into a concrete plan of action.

It is not always easy to get the right people in this sector. Every attempt has been made to create a team, each member of which has relevant skills, integrity, compassion for the less fortunate in society and a deep commitment to the cause of empowering the underprivileged. By patiently waiting for the right person rather than rushing in to engage the first available person, we were able to build an excellent team. All of them have devoted themselves to the cause well beyond the call of duty. Just to take one out of several such instances, on one occasion, Vidya Jayakrishnan, our manager in Pune, worked late into the night on the eve of a major surgery so that the Foundation's work did not suffer.

3

Helping Government Schools

Education is a huge field, involving a vast array of rather complicated issues. While not ignoring the older age groups, the Foundation decided to prioritize elementary education. Both common sense and empirical evidence from around the world, particularly the experience of East Asian countries in the latter half of the twentieth century, indicate the vital importance of this educational stage. Unfortunately, until recently in India, it was precisely this level that did not get the attention it deserved. We see all around us the cumulative effect of this neglect in the millions of illiterate adults and many more who are 'literate' only in government statistics.

Happily, free and compulsory education is now a fundamental right for every child in India between six and fourteen years of age, and Parliament—in the midst of all its shenanigans—has had the wisdom to enact the Right to Education (RTE) Act. It is now the state's duty to fulfil this constitutional mandate. But the magnitude and the complexity of this national goal demands active participation of civil society to complement and supplement the state's efforts.

Perhaps the most challenging issue is the low level of education being imparted in government or municipal schools where the majority of children from economically weak background go. And this despite the fact that the budgetary allocation for Sarva Shiksha Abhiyan, the government's flagship scheme for implementing RTE, have more than doubled—from Rs 26,169 crore in 2009–2010 to Rs 55,746 crore in 2011–2012. Analysts like Yamini Aiyar and Ambrish Dongre of Accountability Initiative, Centre for Policy Research, have taken a close look at the phenomenon and come to the clear conclusion that pouring more money alone is not the solution. They, and many others, have pointed out that the real goal of right to education is to build an education system focused on quality and achieving learning outcomes for children. This requires the education bureaucracy to be attuned to the learning needs of children and to develop appropriate pedagogical strategies to meet them. In short, the state has yet to develop the capacity to deliver all the goals of the RTE Act.

And so TMF conducted a search for outstanding NGOs working to improve the quality of education in government schools. Fortunately, we were eminently successful in locating several such NGOs working towards this objective. There are many different ways in which our partners are pursuing this aim.

As is well-known, a large number of even not so well-off parents, particularly in urban India, prefer to send their children to fee-paying private schools rather than to municipal schools even when the latter provide free education. One reason parents give for this is that they want their children to have an English-medium education. Many educationists are unhappy with this trend because they are convinced that a child's primary education should be in his or her mother tongue for him or her to truly grasp and meaningfully operate fundamental concepts. But these parents have based their assessment on market demand and are convinced that English education is vital for their children's future. To deal with this situation, authorities in a few cities are now introducing English as the medium of instruction in some of their schools. However, they do not always have sufficient number of teachers with the necessary English language competence. Faced with this dilemma, education departments in Mumbai and Pune have invited reputed NGOs to run a few of their English-medium schools. Under this arrangement, the municipal corporation provides the infrastructure—the building, electricity, water, security, mid-day meals, uniforms, books—but the NGOs provide their own teachers and anything else it decides to bring in to improve the quality of education. Three of these NGOs are among TMF's outstanding partners: Akanksha, Aseema and Muktangan.

The schools run by these NGOs, according to our assessment and that of municipal authorities, are providing very good quality education and these children are clearly making better progress than those in normal municipal schools. Each of these NGOs have clearly conceptualized educational philosophy based on sound pedagogic principles, combined with rich experience and above all sensitive concern about the special needs of underprivileged children.

Aseema

Aseema runs several schools. Since 2008, we have partnered with it in the running of the Pali Chimbai Municipal School, Mumbai. Its 600 students include the two young stars of the Oscar-winning film, *Slumdog Millionaire.* While good fortune has smiled on these two, other children continue to live in conditions familiar to anybody who has ever visited some of the most difficult slums of Mumbai. The Aseema-run school provides them with an entirely different environment: 'safe, vibrant and full of learning opportunities' as rightly claimed by the NGO in a recent report to us.

'This is our home'

Frequent visits to the school by TMF personnel have confirmed the effectiveness of the Activity Based Learning approach adopted by Aseema and of its emphasis on the child's personal growth. One has noted with admiration their encouragement of the children to think for themselves and to have a say in the way their school operates. Above all, to quote our Mumbai-based executive, Swati Samant, 'The teachers in the school teach with a lot of love and compassion.'

Aseema and Tech Mahindra

The Tech Mahindra Foundation has been a part of Aseema's journey for over five years. As a donor and supporter, TMF has been instrumental in helping Aseema realize its vision of quality education for underprivileged children. At Aseema, we strongly believe that all children have limitless potential. By offering them a nurturing and stimulating educational environment, we aim to help our children realize all that they are capable of. TMF has been a partner in this process and has encouraged us to work towards excellence.

The Aseema schools have many co-curricular activities like art, judo, sports, music, dance, cinema and theatre, work experience, computers and library time. They recently introduced the Resource Room classes to facilitate the love for learning. This specially designed Resource Room is a very interesting place, full of learning material. Each child decides what they want to do. For this, the children prepare their own monthly plan for how they want to utilize this facility: they do activities related to English, maths, geography, history, general knowledge, art and so on.

> TMF has consistently supported our Primary classes in a municipal school. These classes ensure that children from extremely vulnerable backgrounds receive opportunities to build a strong academic foundation and grow holistically.
>
> Our partnership with TMF has been extremely rewarding. The guidance and feedback we have received from them over the years has helped us build stronger programmes for our children. They have made a significant impact on the lives of our children and we are grateful for their support.
>
> Dilbur Parakh, Chairperson and Trustee, Aseema

To get a feel of the long term impact of the years spent with Aseema, I met some former students. Each of them came from families where parents were barely literate and each is

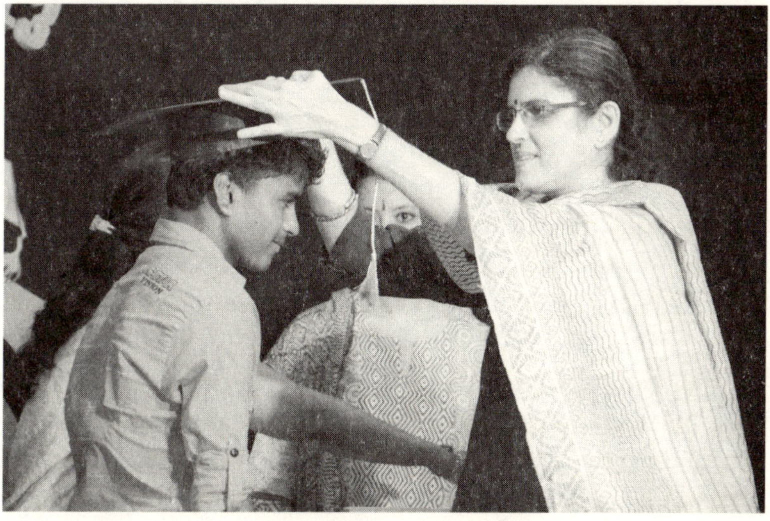

Dilbur felicitating a proud Aseema graduate

now determined and equipped to take on the challenges which lie ahead. Sushmita, one of the academic stars of the school, declared that her aspiration was to be a doctor but said she would happily be a teacher in Aseema if she did not make it to a medical college. In either case, she was committed to serving the community. Exuding heart-warming sincerity she attributed her success to her seventh standard Aseema teacher, whom she lauded as her 'inspiration and mentor'. And then there was this eighteen-year-old boy, who was compelled by family circumstances to transfer from a private fee-paying school to Aseema, and drew a clear distinction between the two schools: 'There they teach us just to get marks; here they teach us to be good people, how you can help others, how you can achieve your dreams.' The son of a driver, he hopes one day to do hotel management. Particularly enjoyable was my meeting with Ashish Gaekwad, a young man in his late teens, who is already seeing his dreams come true. Encouraged by Aseema and blessed with exceptional talent, he is on his way to becoming a film-maker, having received a two-year scholarship from a famous film director/producer to study in his institute.

The higher amount now available to the Foundation for disbursement has enabled it to make a greater contribution to bringing quality education to municipal schools. It has now chosen some schools for total adoption. Greatly impressed with Aseema's work, it has not only adopted the Pali Chimbai Municipal School but also joined the NGO in adopting yet another school, the Kherwadi Municipal School in Bandra East. TMF accepted Aseema's proposal to take over the entire school from the first standard to the sixth with 178 children in 2013–14. The plan is to add a class every year till the school reaches tenth standard.

Muktangan

Muktangan runs seven English-medium municipal schools of which TMF has supported one. Its most distinctive feature is the dedication and effectiveness of the teachers who are drawn from the same slum communities as the students and who—thanks to an exceedingly well thought out and very intensive training programme—are able to run English-medium classes though they themselves are products of Marathi-medium schools. The children display high confidence levels and are exposed to many extracurricular activities. Some years ago, they stunned an audience in Mumbai's prestigious National Centre for Performing Arts with a brilliant rendering of songs from *The Sound of Music* with the help of Johannes Steinbender, an Austrian conductor who specializes in training children's choirs.

We had invited an experienced team of external evaluators to assess the Muktangan model. This is what they had to say in their conclusion:

'Yes, we too can do it'

This model lays great emphasis on child centred learning; children are treated as active learners and teachers facilitate this learning. Parents are perceived as a source of strength and support and treated as equal partners at Muktangan. The teachers are highly motivated.

Muktangan's experience of working with Tech Mahindra Foundation (TMF)

Tech Mahindra Foundation began supporting Muktangan in 2007 and was one of its earliest donors. The support has continued over six consecutive years. Such a long period of support is extremely significant for a budding, struggling organization like ours, which then left us free to concentrate on our core activity of education. The programme could also be strategized, planned and implemented more effectively.

Even when the support was to end, we were warned about it and the support was tapered off over two years, allowing us adequate time to make alternative arrangements. Very few donor organizations manifest this consistency and mature understanding of the NGO's needs.

Besides the financial support, TMF kept themselves abreast of Muktangan's development and growth over the years. Mr Khanna and the staff had periodic meetings with us in meaningful discussions which helped us further refine our strategies and programme. They have been appreciative of what we achieved, empathetic to what we could not and, while holding us accountable for the attainment of targets and proper utilization of funds, remained practically flexible when circumstances demanded some adjustment.

Muktangan is grateful to TMF for their support, confidence and faith in its programme.

Sunil Mehta
Managing Trustee, Muktangan

Akanksha

Yet another organization that has accepted the challenge of running a few municipal schools is Akanksha. A visit to its schools is always a delightful experience. In the Bopodi school in Pune, about 250 little children from Junior KG to second standard are taking a giant leap forward from their non-English-speaking and often illiterate parents into an English-medium early-education environment—one that could match any of the fancy fee-paying private schools. Teachers enjoy a terrific rapport with the little children. Games, yoga, art and craft, siesta time are all part of the Akanksha curriculum.

Like Muktangan, this NGO, too, has shown

exceptional ability to reach out to parents and make them feel that they are an integral part of the marvellous educational experience of their children.

A spin-off effect is the impact on behaviour patterns in the society from which the parents and children come. A striking illustration of this is the fact that 90 per cent of the fathers turn up for the parents' meeting.

So popular has the school become in the Bopodi neighbourhood that Akanksha has had to resort to a lottery to determine new admissions.

When our partnership with Akanksha began in Pune, we had the feeling that a major challenge would be to build a productive mutually beneficial rapport with the concerned officials of the Pune Municipal Corporation. Significant progress has been made in this area though—like anybody working in this field anywhere in the country—one has to accept certain amount of bureaucratic delays.

'Mom sees me off to school'

Akanksha's reputation and network built by the indomitable Shaheen Mistri and her colleagues results in highly qualified young people being attracted to work with it, both as full-time teachers and as part-time volunteers.

'I know the answer'

Akanksha has ambitious plans for the future of the school. It began with just KG. But each year it adds one new standard. They have reached the second standard but propose to go all the way to the tenth standard and perhaps eventually even extend to the twelfth, or what in Maharashtra is termed the Junior College stage. There is every reason to believe that they will achieve their goal and the school will no doubt be the pride of the community.

Under the five-year rule, our support to this particular school has had to be phased out but we have now joined Akanksha in adopting the Wadibunder Municipal School in Mumbai. This school was started with one class of junior KG with thirty-five students. The school will grow to full capacity in the year 2023–24 and will reach out to 420 students by adding a grade each year with thirty-five students.

These organizations have collectively struggled to get the municipal corporations of Mumbai and Pune to ensure sustainability by providing the same level of per-child funding support as they budget for schools run by themselves.

Some Other Partners

A different approach has been adopted by another partner of ours, the Naandi Foundation, in Mumbai. Instead of taking over the running of the municipal schools and appointing teachers, Naandi has undertaken to train and assist municipal teachers in a certain number of English-medium schools. It has introduced in the schools a team of teaching assistants who are trained to facilitate, handle classroom management and delivery of lessons. There is a comprehensive teacher assessment tool which captures all the elements of the role of the teacher. This helps Naandi provide quality training to municipal teachers on skills involving innovative teaching techniques, classroom management etc.

A project entitled 'Supporting Equitable Access for Girls to Education' run by the Centre for British Teachers (CfBT) Education Services in Hyderabad has a wider scope than the Naandi programme but shares with it the approach of improving skills of the existing government-school teachers. The ten schools covered are Kasturba Gandhi Balika Vidyalayas (KGBV). It is an exercise in public–private partnership (or PPP), involving engagement with Sarva Shiksha Abhiyan and the government of Andhra Pradesh.

This project is a response to the request from the government. The design of this pilot project is innovative and addresses the issues of equity, access, quality and rights awareness in an integrated manner. TMF and the KGBV Society make almost an equal contribution to support this project.

A baseline assessment on the four skills (listening, speaking, reading and writing) of English for grades six, seven, eight and nine revealed that all the students needed to improve on the four skills to improve their proficiency in the language. The interest level in listening and speaking activities is found to be quite high and a lot of interventions have been planned for this. In order to provide effective teacher support, CfBT trainers are using the demonstration technique to train students directly in the presence of English teachers of the school. The teachers have also been cooperative.

While the TMF's support of Aseema, Akanksha, Muktangan, Naandi, the Centre for British Teachers (CfBT) Education Services and a new initiative in Chennai is all in English-medium schools, one of our partners, the Bombay Community Public Trust, has a project to improve the teaching of English in Marathi-medium schools. The Trust, with the help of Tata Interactive Systems (for curriculum design, writing, music composition, graphics and technical integration) and Muktangan (for conceptualizing the content), has created interactive DVDs that follow the Maharashtra government's prescribed English curriculum. Knowing that the teaching of English is very difficult for the teachers in vernacular schools—many

Dear Mr Khanna and Vidya,
I am immensely grateful to TMF for the excellent support you gave to this initiative when it was in its nascent stage, and when we really had no performance to show. Your faith and support has been a major factor in helping us to get started, and getting the initial momentum. As we progress now, I want this to stay on record as the invaluable contribution to the e.teach Project from Tech Mahindra Foundation, through your understanding & support.

Under this 'e.teach' Project, colourful, animated, and interactive DVDs have been scientifically prepared to teach the prescribed Maharashtra Govt vernacular-school curriculum, using a TV with a DVD-player. These are then replicated in large numbers and given free to urban and rural schools.

These animated DVDs hold the rapt attention of the young students.

By encouraging talking, singing and acting in the classroom children develop confidence in speaking to one another, with proper diction.

The Project was launched in 2010. In the school-year 2012–13 it had reached over 5,600 primary school students in Mumbai, and over 6,000 children in the rural Wada Taluka of Maharashtra.

With warm regards, and sincerest thanks,

Astad Parakh, Bombay Community Public Trust

of whom are themselves not quite fluent in English—we found this to be an excellent teaching aid. The visuals consist of beautiful and apt pictorial representation of the text. The audio has excellent and absolutely clear articulation, something that should be of great help not only to students but teachers as well. And the students seem to be finding it both enjoyable and useful. But I understand from Astad Parakh, who has worked hard to disseminate the programme, that it has been an uphill task persuading municipal teachers to use it. There has been greater success in private schools run by charitable bodies for the economically disadvantaged.

Distinct from our work to improve English language learning in government schools is our work with the NGO Katha. There will be much more on its Lab School in a subsequent chapter. Here we need to record how the learnings from this school are used to improve the quality of teaching in municipal schools. To quote from Katha's report, 'The Katha Lab School has always been the ground for innovation and creativity . . . Katha's philosophy, story pedagogy, learning components such as integrated teaching, continuous assessment and development of teaching–learning material have been shared during the workshops. Senior teachers from here were resource people at the MCD Principals Meet where fifty principals were brought together by Katha for a capacity-building exercise.'

In September 2013, the Ops Committee approved a proposal to use technology to spread Katha's message to a larger number of municipal school teachers. The KREATE Cloud Guru pilot will provide basic computer training to 750 teachers in seventy-five MCD (the erstwhile Muncipal Corporation of Delhi) schools with the dual aim of orienting them on accessing educational content online as well as convincing them about the usefulness of computers in saving time and improving student performance.

The pilot will also test conditions in MCD schools—in terms of IT and physical infrastructure, teacher interest and engagement—for a roll-out of a more intensive Cloud Guru training programme. Under the pilot programme, Katha will also create an online resource of eBooks and videos and make them available on a special website—www.padhopyarese.net—and test mobile/online technologies for providing support to teachers and students on accessing Katha's online educational content. The findings from the pilot will be incorporated into the design of the larger Katha KREATE Cloud Guru project that Katha intends to submit to TMF in 2014.

Some of our NGOs run enrichment programmes within municipal schools. Two of them, Door Step and Swadhar in Pune, seek to improve the reading skills of all children, while one, SARD in Delhi, runs a remedial programme for children lagging behind. The fourth, Disha, is offering teaching–learning support to four municipal schools through resource centres, classroom-based support and building capacity of teachers. We have been particularly happy with their resource centre activities which include activities from textbooks, painting, sports, singing and dancing. The head of the organization is a dedicated Gandhian and this is reflected in the nature of some of the activities included to develop creativity and interest amongst the students.

Door Step is headed by well-known social worker, Rajani Paranjpe. It has been successfully conducting the Reading Class programme for the last eight years in various public schools. In 1999, it started this programme with just ten PMC (Pune Municipal Corporation) primary schools; today, it is working in seventy-six schools, forty-seven in PMC and twenty-nine in PCMC (Pimpri Chinchwad Municipal Corporation) with the support of several sponsors, including TMF.

To understand the impact of the programme, Door Step has been conducting a reading ability test twice every year. One test is conducted at the beginning of the academic year and the second at the end of the academic year. Among fourth standard children in schools where reading classes were not conducted, it was found that only 50 per cent were able to read any book or written matter without difficulty. But 85 per cent children of the same grade exposed to reading classes could read the same book or written matter without any difficulty. Besides, there are other benefits: the attention spans of students increase, they are not listless and their reading speed also increases.

The Society for All Round Development, better known by its acronym SARD, runs a comprehensive remedial programme in several municipal schools in Delhi. It Chief Executive Sudhir Bhatnagar has built a strong team with a good reputation for enrichment of formal education through remedial teaching in MCD schools.

SARD has developed a good understanding with all stakeholders: the school principals, teachers and parents. Its work has led to the improvement of enrolment and attendance with a significantly reduced dropout rate in the thirty schools where its work was supported by TMF. The learning levels in reading, writing and numeracy of over a thousand children in what they call 'Anand-dayi kakshas' have improved. To widen children's horizons, it has book clubs, bal-melas, bal-diwas, environment day celebrations, creative writing workshops, story telling workshops, exposure visits, art camps and so on.

With TMF's assistance, a strong Management Information System has been established to track the socio-economic status, pedagogical progress, migration, learning achievement, dropout figures, disability status and parental involvement etc.

Under the five-year rule, the partnership with SARD ended with the academic year 2012–13. But it has built a good relationship with international funding agencies and TMF's withdrawal should not adversely affect its work.

We were happy to have the scope of our work in government schools expanded with the arrival of the Mahindra Satyam Foundation into our family. It managed six so-called KidSmart Early Learning centres in Hyderabad. This programme utilized software developed by IBM designed to give young children who are attending pre-school centres and primary schools an enriching and stimulating environment. Following the five-year rule, these too have been phased out.

A new partner, Association for Promoting Social Action (APSA), joined us in Hyderabad in 2013 to continue an earlier programme of Mahindra Satyam Foundation: Multimedia Enabled Learning Centres in Government Schools.

The seeds of APSA were sown in 1976, when a group of about eight young people decided to intervene to improve the exploitative conditions under which the coolies (loading and unloading workers) of the Secunderabad railway station worked.

The objective of the APSA project is to improve the quality of education and bridge the divide between government schools and private schools in terms of digital literacy.

Broadly the following aspects are to be covered:

- Ensure ICT education among the students
- Create awareness of multimedia learning among community
- Prepare students for today's reality, and
- Ensure a better future for students

Sahitya Reddi, our Hyderabad-based executive had this to say while submitting the proposal:

I recommend that we should support this programme as the centres have been well appreciated by the school managements and also respective District Education Officers. The students are also making best utilization of the centres especially to learn maths, science and English.

Another partner, Prardhana Charitable Trust, has been instrumental in construction of three government primary schools in Hyderabad. In the past two years, the Trust has been trying to raise the quality of education in these three schools, each having about 200 children from classes one to five.

One of our partners in Bangalore, Dhwani, has produced innovative and effective teaching–learning materials in Kannada. Over the last three years, we have been very impressed by the vision and intelligence of Shivananda Hombal who leads this programme. Through this endeavour, exciting educational material for Kannada language has been created to supplement the prescribed text books in schools.

Significantly, Dhwani largely accepts one self-imposed limitation. It is not particularly fond of participating in a training programme which the teachers must attend compulsorily. Dhwani rightly believes that a teacher is more likely to use innovative materials and methods only if she/he is at the programme voluntarily. If a teacher attends because she is ordered to do so, she will rapidly lapse into her traditional mode of teaching. Innovation, the NGO believes, requires a higher order of motivation which has to come from within.

All printed materials are uploaded to the Dhwani website and these are freely available for use even by teachers, parents and students.

Recent Developments

Room to Read, an international NGO with which partnership has just begun, establishes school libraries and stocks them with English books, local-language books, and some of their original Room to Read titles. Brightly coloured furniture, puzzles and games foster a child-friendly environment.

This project promotes the habit of reading by:

- Training and supporting teachers and librarians for three years
- Providing books and educational materials to schools for three years
- Collaborating with schools to ensure effective and sufficient time to read
- Supporting schools to set up a learning environment that encourages reading
- Engaging families and communities, including meetings with parents, committees, and literacy and reading awareness events

Our executive's assessment made the proposal irresistible:

The Room to Read library is a very attractive room in the midst of badly maintained Municipal School classrooms. It has brightly coloured furniture, educative posters on the walls and shelves filled with books. It serves as a big attraction for the Municipal School children to come to school. The library has age-appropriate, culturally-relevant reading materials that allow the children to develop a habit of reading and increase literacy levels. All the books are levelled and the teacher keeps a track of the progress of each child from one level to another. Apart from the reading, the children also enjoy other activities like drawing, writing, singing etc. in the library. Training of teachers and librarians, and engaging families and communities, ensures sustainability of the libraries and for the children to be able to access them and receive their benefits long after Room to Read's three years of support is over. The Municipal teachers and the headmasters are involved right from the beginning and hence I observed a great sense of ownership towards the library in the Municipal staff.

TMF recently moved into Chennai in a big way. In collaboration with the Corporation of Chennai, we have initiated an English teacher training programme for English medium corporation schools. At present, the level of English teaching is very poor. In a pilot project, 100 teachers have been selected from about twenty school. They will undergo intensive training through the Cambridge English Language Assessment group. This is a non-profit venture of Cambridge University and is internationally renowned for its English teaching and assessment. The implementing agency in India is the Cambridge University Press.

This is a very promising pilot project with the expectation of steady expansion in years to come.

The background to this partnership is the following report of our manager, Mamatha Esteves:

There are 285 corporation schools in the city of Chennai under the jurisdiction of Commissioner and Joint Commissioner of Education. Of them 85 have classrooms which are supposed to be taught in English and hence the so called English-medium schools. The teachers in these schools have not been specifically trained in English to cater to the children's need of studying in English medium. The subjects are taught by the Tamil teachers in the local language much against the parents' expectations of their children being taught in English.

There has been a continuous outflow of children from these schools to low-cost English-medium private schools. The government is struggling with the issue of retention and is trying their best to get the children back . . .

In the chapter on our NGO partners in Bangalore I shall have much to say about the amazing work done by Parikrma. (Yes, that is how they spell their name and not, as one would expect, Parikrama!) Here, I will introduce the launching of a very important venture which will hopefully help in improving the quality of education in not only some other NGO schools but also in government schools. TMF has decided to support the Parikrma Education Transformation Centre.

The following extract from their proposal gives a good idea about the aspiration of the Centre:

The curriculum that is available through various syllabi like the State Boards, ICSE, CBSE and the IB etc. are not bad but the understanding of this curriculum and the reason why it is has been framed this way has not been looked into by teachers. There is a big divide between the educationists (the education theorists) and the practitioners (school operators and teachers). It is taken for granted that the teachers do not need to ask questions but follow the prescribed content and that has been the trend all these years. They are also therefore creating the culture of followership which is transacted into rote learning in the classrooms. If the teachers on the other hand were taught to reason, to understand why the curriculum has been designed in the manner it has, what is the synergy between the curriculum and the developmental stages of the child, we believe that there would be a lot of sensitive and intelligent teaching in the schools.

What is striking about the project is that it will also cover training not only of teachers but also of principals and all others involved in administering the school system.

Though well-versed in theory, there will be in the ETC greater emphasis on practice. Parikrma has, in its existing schools, demonstrated its ability to successfully inculcate in teachers the value of and the road to experiential creative learning. Some of the other features it hopes to replicate—with improvements through research and help of other experts—are:

- Classroom organization and management
- Pupil assessment
- Differentiation
- Experiments with critical thinking
- Working with community and
- Professional reflection and personal commitment

Preparation and planning for ETC has begun, dominated by action research.

Even more ambitious is the East Delhi Municipal Corporation (EDMC) In-Service Teacher Education Institute, a truly challenging task taken up by TMF. Undertaken in close collaboration with EDMC's education wing, it has the potential for greatly improving the quality of teaching in municipal schools in the areas. Chapter 5 will give details of this venture

One of the most popular activities TMF has devised as its contribution to better quality teaching in Delhi's municipal schools of Delhi is the Shikshak Samman Awards. This has become a flagship programme and deserves a brief chapter by itself.

4

Shikshak Samman Awards: One of TMF's Flagship Programmes

Before it was split into three smaller corporations, the Municipal Corporation of Delhi (MCD) was responsible for running about 1800 schools with almost a million children. It is the 20,000 or so teachers of these schools who play the central role in shaping the minds of these children. Many such teachers are working with great determination and dedication in the face of several daunting challenges to ensure that their students receive a decent education. They deserve recognition and encouragement by the civil society. And so, the Foundation in 2008 instituted the Shikshak Samman Awards (SSA) to honour outstanding teachers and principals working in the national capital's municipal schools. In subsequent years, a decision was taken to concentrate on teachers.

Over the years, SSA has become one of TMF's flagship programmes and has continued even after the trifurcation of the MCD. It has involved very hard and committed work by two successive senior TMF executives: Priyali Prakash and Dr Nuzhat Ali.

> As we strive to build a more just and prosperous India, the nation is specially indebted to those teachers who have the responsibility of teaching children from under privileged background. It is the commitment of the teachers in municipal schools which has the potential to transform the lives of these children.
>
> Keshub Mahindra

The selection process is transparent, independent and fair and has been hailed as such. The jury, comprising eminent educationists, base their decision on the application forms, passages which the teachers are asked to write in the Foundation office on the day of the interview, interviews, observation of classroom performance and assessment of principals.

The distinguished panel of jurists are requested to keep, *inter alia*, the following criteria in mind: innovation and motivation in teaching, empathy for underprivileged, constant endeavour at self-improvement and efforts at reducing dropouts.

Besides a cash award and a Teaching Learning Material kit, the awardees are given an opportunity for further professional development through programmes like a residential training retreat and workshops with experienced educationists as resource persons.

Many of these teachers are barely in their twenties and have a long career ahead, full of opportunities to mould several

A good teacher is a perennial learner

generations of students. They are full of youthful energy and idealism. Namita Bhagat, belonging to the 2010–11 batch of Shikshak Samman Awardees, is one such young, energetic and vibrant teacher. An MA in English, she has also acquired MEd. and BElEd (Bachelor of Elementary Education) degrees. Her impressive knowledge of what constitutes good teaching was clearly reflected in her application form. That her knowledge was not merely theoretical was obvious in her responses to the jury's searching queries. Seeing her in action in class was a sheer delight. Her rapport with children was just amazing.

Given the fact that they have decided to devote their lives to teaching underprivileged children, it is not surprising that many outstanding municipal school teachers take keen interest in the well being of the community from which these children come. Mohammad Fatima, who teaches in an Urdu-medium school, keeps in close touch with the parents, most of whom are small vendors and daily wage workers.

Namita mesmerizing her students

Fatima

Even before we saw the reports of the study by the brilliant Harvard economist Raj Chetty—winner of the John Bates Clark Medal, often called 'the baby Nobel'—on the life-long impact of a good kindergarten experience, we were aware of the critical importance of early childhood education. It was decided from the second year of the SSA scheme awards to reserve two awards for nursery teachers. We found our decision vindicated by the outstanding quality of many of these. When the Tech Mahindra team entrusted with classroom observation saw Asha Rani, who had been selected by the interview board, at work she was enacting a story before thirty odd four-year-olds who clearly adored her. Though highly qualified, she has deliberately chosen to teach at the nursery level. Her principal says, 'Because of the beauty of her class, the school looks beautiful.' Equally delightful was the visit to the class of Anju Kaur.

Asha Rani (above) and Anju Kaur (below) with their adoring little ones

We also recognize the importance of arts and physical education and have one award reserved for each category. Thus we were happy when Kusum Malasi was selected in 2010. We had been aware of her marvellous work as a music teacher. The performances put up by her students have received wide acclaim. She is a great advocate of the role of the arts in education—music, dance, drama, painting, theatre, indeed of all forms of creative expression. In her interview, she shared her distress at music being given a back seat in the face of resource crunch or infrastructural problems. In her soft and gentle voice, she says she regrets music being perceived only as a source of entertainment and not integrated into the regular school curriculum.

The Shikshak Samman awardees have spoken of how recognition by an independent agency like TMF has been a source of immense inspiration, motivating them to do even better in the years to come. Pradeep Kumar, one of the teachers honoured in the very first year of the scheme, revealed that he was deeply moved by

Pradeep Kumar

the very use of the term *samman* by TMF and that the award was the turning point in his life.

In a similar vein, Brajesh Kumar Jadon, awardee of the 2009–10 batch writes, 'This samman is one of a kind, one that rewards as well as challenges. It undoubtedly carries recognition for our passion and dedication towards teaching; it also imposes a responsibility to do more and to do it better. Just a look at our award connects us to our children and what we do with them.'

More than one awardee was thrilled that the award was not restricted to a cheque but gave them an opportunity to grow professionally. To quote Sangeeta Yadav of the 2010–11 batch, 'We have a skill. The workshops and trainings organized under the Samman programme give us a chance to enrich that skill and help us to become better teachers every day.'

It is our hope that these awards will inspire not only the awardees but the municipal system as a whole to give better education to the children of our capital, making an important contribution to our society's future.

In the meanwhile, we have sought to highlight the role of the main pillar of the edifice: the much maligned teacher. The fact is that though many teachers in government/municipal schools are indeed disappointing, there are thousands of them across the country who are doing their best often in very trying circumstances. They have earned our respect and admiration. TMF is now planning to replicate SSA in other cities.

> Henry Adams: A teacher affects eternity; he can never tell where his influence stops.

5

ITEI and ARISE: Meeting Two Formidable Challenges

I. In-Service Teacher Education Institute (ITEI)

After the trifurcation of the Municipal Corporation of Delhi, the East Delhi Municipal Corporation (EDMC) is now a separate unit. It runs 390 primary schools in Shahadra North and Shahadra South catering to about 2.4 lakh children. Approximately, 4000 teachers are involved in this mammoth task of ensuring education for the most marginalized children of east Delhi. As we saw in the previous chapter, some of these teachers are outstanding. Unfortunately, this cannot be said of a large number of other teachers. They are academically well-qualified and now reasonably well-paid. However, something is missing, a factor that is responsible for the widely recognized poor quality of teaching-learning in these schools. The EDMC's education department was determined to rectify the situation. TMF offered to help. This is the background of the public-private partnership project between the two institutions to set up an In-Service Teacher Education Institute (ITEI). The partnership project was signed between EDMC and TMF on 13 March 2013.

Before initiating the project, a lot of work went into developing an understanding about the needs of the teachers and the system. A need analysis study was conducted by a consulting group. After this, a core group was formed by the then EDMC commissioner. The group, comprising members of EDMC and TMF, worked on resource mapping and the project design document. It was decided to set up an ITEI in one of the east Delhi schools.

It was envisaged that the project will be implemented collaboratively over five years with a vision to achieve the following objectives:

1. Develop a fully functional and effective ITEI
2. Enable an environment of quality education by enhancing knowledge, skill and attitude of all the stakeholders, especially the teachers
3. Build favourable environment for ensuring systemic reforms through ITEI

It was planned that the ITEI will use modern innovative pedagogical practices and IT enabled educational services. The Foundation identified a team of academic experts and resource persons to develop systems and processes to run an effective ITEI. The first year was identified as the preparatory phase.

An excellent rapport was established between all the partners under the committed leadership of TMF's CEO Loveleen Kacker and EDMC Education Director K. Vijayan assisted by Foundation's Education Manager Nuzhat Ali and EDMC officials.

The institute established contact with a number of research and related institutions ranging from Eklavya, NCERT, SCERT, National Museum and universities to the Centre for Science and Environment and the Vikram A. Sarabhai Community Science Centre. These agencies have shown interest in sharing their resources, both human and material, with ITEI for bringing quality changes in the EDMC school system. ITEI didn't limit itself to institutions but also networked with young research scholars and individual educationists for them to contribute to the manuals and the training process for ITEI.

It was planned that manuals would be developed for the teaching of Hindi and mathematics. In addition, one induction manual would be developed for the newly recruited teachers. These manuals would focus on areas identified on the basis of the shared vision and inputs of teachers, educational experts, EDMC officials, other stakeholders and needs' analysis findings. The design would largely focus on 'transformational objectives' such as:

- Increasing motivational levels, building and enriching a positive self-concept
- Building climate of inquiry and making teachers reflective practitioners
- Evolving educational professionals who are receptive, perceptive, innovative and dynamic

Several meetings were held to discuss the basic issues and assumptions about teaching and learning that need to be addressed in the manuals.

The team working on the manual for the teaching of mathematics found that the teachers were not familiar with the rationale and philosophy behind the new textbooks based on National Curriculum Framework (NCF) 2005. Hence, despite being professionally qualified and experienced, many were not comfortable with transacting the textbooks in the classroom.

Keeping in view the above findings and the recommendations of NCF 2005 for teaching mathematics at primary level, the team is working on four modules. Effort is being made to use local examples revolving around the children's real life experiences. The concepts are explained in easy language using activities involving everyday objects.

A detailed data base is being prepared of all EDMC teachers which will include information regarding their qualification, experience, training needs, training already attended, awards won and innovations (if any). This information base once ready will help not only in organizing the training programme but also in providing on-site support, counselling personalized consultations, mentoring, peer-coaching, lateral exchange, and organization of study circles for providing specific and focused assistance to schools as per their requirement.

Stakeholders' Capacity Building Programme

EDMC has 113 English-medium schools. These schools face a number of challenges. The first training programme of ITEI was on 'Developing Proficiency in English Teaching', in which thirty teachers participated. This training was a precursor to a series of intensive capacity building sessions to be conducted in the future. The programmes aim at creating a pool of teachers who could later on work as Master trainers for ITEI's future programmes.

In order to build ownership and to develop common understanding about the roles, mission, and the function of the ITEI, a one-day Vision Building Programme was organized for top EDMC officials.

Setting Up Monitoring Mechanism

The project manager in close coordination with the TMF education manager and the head of research & extension, EDMC, is responsible for monitoring ITEI.

In order to approve, supervise and give direction to the academic work and various activities undertaken for realizing the goals of the project, a Project Academic Council (PAC), consisting of distinguished experts from reputed institutes has been constituted.

For overall supervision of project activities, the Project Steering Committee (PSC) has been constituted. It will take stock of the progress of the project and formulate the policies and provisions with regard to ITEI administration. It will also facilitate the overall change management process for bringing about systemic reform. The PSC, co-chaired by the EDMC commissioner and TMF CEO, will meet twice a year.

In a very short span of time, the project team has not only stabilized itself in the EDMC system but also built strong and cordial linkages with several leading institutions to accomplish the project's objectives. But TMF recognizes that there are a lot of challenges ahead.

II. All-Round Improvement in School Education (ARISE)

TMF has always been devoted to the all-round improvement of schools in which its partner NGOs work. With greater resources now being available, it has been able to increase its support to the work of these partners. But special mention needs to be made of two initiatives launched in 2013.

Lab School

This 'ARISE' exercise is in tandem with ITEI.

The Lab School is based on an agreement between TMF and Vidya & Child run by the Jayaprakash Narayan Memorial Trust (JNMT) team, about whom we shall have much more to say later in the book. They have been selected by the Foundation to work on the Lab School project due to their expertise in level-based curriculum planning and transaction for meeting the differentiated needs of children from underprivileged background. The EDMC school complex where ITEI is located will also function as a Lab School. This school will be used as practical ground for the actualization of learnings gained at the ITEI and institutionalize best practices identified to enhance developmental opportunities for children. This school will also be provided after-school programmes (running various hobby sessions, life skills development and co-curricular activities) so as to ensure quality development opportunities to marginalized children.

Specific focus areas of the intervention under the Lab School project include:

1. Using the Building as a Learning Aid (BALA)
2. Community Outreach Programme
   - Improvement in attendance
   - Building stronger relationships with parents for ensuring sustained involvement in child's education
3. Improvement in quality of education
4. Teacher trainings
5. Fresh focus on
   - Life skills
   - Creative programme
   - Sports

Kasturba Balika Vidyalaya

Kasturba Balika Vidyalaya (KBV) is a government-aided senior secondary school for girls. Situated in south Delhi, it was established in 1944 by Harijan Sewak Sangh (HSS) to commemorate Kasturba Gandhi and to provide quality education to girls from underprivileged families.

Shyam Suri, a retired IAS official and manager of the school, and HSS officials approached TMF to help improve infrastructural and learning facilities for the students. TMF has taken up the challenge enthusiastically.

To quote from a note on ARISE prepared by Nuzhat Ali, 'This intervention of TMF is continuously impacting various domains of the school: physical dimension (infrastructure/physical facilities) cognitive dimension (related to enabling learning) social dimension (in terms of relationships, values—specially equity—and the emotional environment of classrooms and the school) and organizational dimension (school to be an effectively managed institution linked to the community).'

In this exercise, TMF has sought the collaboration of eminent educationist Prof. Jalaluddin. He has held senior faculty and technical advisory positions at NCERT, several universities, UNESCO and UNDP. He is the founder-trustee of NEEV, a charitable public trust, which is actively engaged in promoting

Prof. A.K. Jalaluddin

educational change through innovation, research and training. Now in his late 70s, he is in indifferent health but it is most inspiring to see him in action in the school along with his young team from NEEV.

An additional vital dimension is brought in by Sakshi, a group which has introduced into the school counselling, life skills and theatre.

To ensure holistic education, TMF has also brought in the Magic Bus, which as we shall see elsewhere specializes in using sports as an important aid to development.

With such an intensive involvement of TMF and its partners, one can certainly hope to see 'All Round Improvement in School Education' in these two schools, which hopefully will act as replicable role models.

6

Educational Initiatives in Pune

Besides partnering with several NGOs endeavouring to improve the quality of education in municipal schools, we have joined hands with some exceptional organizations who work independently of the government system and reach out to particularly vulnerable children.

Due to an earlier tradition referred to in the introductory chapter, Tech Mahindra associates in Pune have played an important role in identifying some very fine NGOs for us to partner. To these have been added several identified by the TMF team both in Pune and elsewhere in Maharashtra. This chapter shall cover most of our partners, past and present, working in and around Pune towards providing education to economically and socially marginalized children. NGOs that provide education to the physically challenged are covered in a separate chapter.

Vanasthali

When we began our quest for new partners in Pune, I sought the advice of somebody introduced to me by an old Pune resident as 'just the person to guide you'—Vijay Kuwalekar, former editor of the famous Marathi newspaper *Sakal.* He had no hesitation in recommending Nirmala Purandare, founder head of Vanasthali.

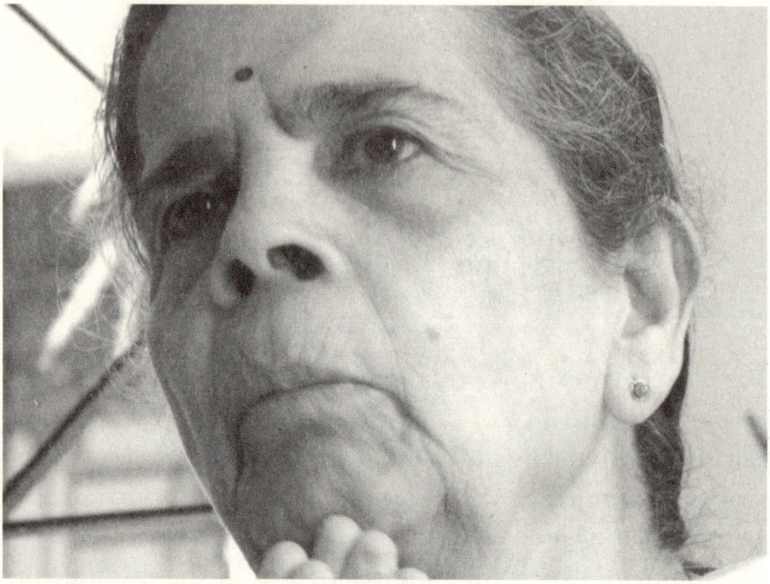

Nirmala Purandare, founder head of Vanasthali

Having been involved in early childhood education because of my work with Pratham, I listened with great admiration to what Nirmala Tai had to say on the subject of balwadis. The way she had taken her work into rural areas, through a process of empowering village women, was most impressive. Vanasthali trains them to run classes which cover both education and entertainment through a wide variety of educational games. She chose for this purpose zila parishad schools, not known for providing holistic education. To quote Vanasthali literature, 'We make rural woman focal point of our activities so that her potentialities are explored and utilized and then these are directed towards child development and improved education of children through Balwadis and hobby classes. Villages lack not only in civic amenities and in formal education facilities, but also in facilities for wholesome recreational activities. When we realized this deprivation, we decided to introduce hobby classes in rural milieu.'

The range of skills covered in their training is astonishing. To quote from their proposal:

1. handicrafts
2. dramatics, story telling
3. puppetry
4. indoor games
5. songs
6. reading
7. drawing and painting
8. gardening
9. nature study and environment protection
10. scientific experiments related to day-to-day life etc.

And then comes the onerous task of introducing these activities in schools totally unaccustomed to such enrichment of children's education.

To understand better Vanasthali's vision, we asked them to spell out the expected outcomes. Their list gave us confidence in the thinking that had gone into conceptualizing the programme. According to them, these classes lead to creativity and imagination; realization of one's own inclinations, likes and dislikes; development of skills in language, expression, communication and handicraft. They inculcate aesthetic sense; increase peer feeling and social skills such as cooperation, discipline, sharing and caring, peace and concentration of mind and help lessen school dropouts. Of course, it was clear that this entire list could not always be realized in practice.

It was gratifying to learn that though Vanasthali had some major foreign supporters, TMF was the first major Indian donor to this programme that simultaneously empowers village women and helps children blossom, deepening their interest in education and widening knowledge of their environment.

Reports from our local executives confirmed that this innovative intervention significantly enhanced children's interest in their school besides adding quality to their learning. Through thirty-one classes across six schools in rural and urban part of Pune, the project supported by TMF impacted around 3800 children.

Karmarveer Bhausaheb Hire (KBH) School

This school was introduced to us by one of our Tech Mahindra colleagues who had been volunteering there for many years. It is a grant-in-aid co-educational Marathi-medium school. It caters to students from low-income families. Our support to the school began with small grants to enable them to buy new uniforms for the girls and sweaters for all the children. This was then extended to notebooks and shoes.

Subsequent visits gave rise to the idea that we could make a significant contribution to improving the quality of the school. It had adequate number of teachers and classrooms but insufficient funds to meet some essential educational requirements. Discussions with the principal led by our Pune executive Vijay gave fresh insights. Following a joint TMF-KBH evaluation it was decided to strengthen the science and computer labs and provide additional resources to the sports section.

Later on one of our visits, the science teacher told us excitedly that the combined impact of upgrading of the science lab and the establishment of the computer lab, has been to transform the teaching of science in the school. He was thrilled to use the LCD facility provided by TMF. He explained that this was particularly useful while studying a topic beyond the children's normal experience. Like children in any well-run school, the students here too are getting accustomed to using the Internet to enrich their information base. On the day of one of our visits, the topic was 'drosera', which I learnt were carnivorous plants! The limited textbook material was enriched by enthusiastic follow-through research by the students. With the sort of modesty one would welcome in any teacher, he declared, 'It is they who teach me now.'

One sometimes hears of educationists complaining about the declining interest in science education in the country. But when I spoke to the tenth standard students of this school, I found a very large number liked science and wanted to pursue it at college level. Some even looked forward to a career in some scientific field. One of the girls declared confidently that she hoped to become a research scientist. Hopefully, facilities provided by TMF have contributed to stimulating this interest.

It was also found that of 1000 or so children in the school, about 300 came from particularly weak economic backgrounds; in a large number of these cases, the parents were daily-wage earners faced with the constant challenge of meeting the family's basic survival needs. It was decided to accept the school's request to provide financial resources to cover the entire expenditure on their education.

The school management informed us with legitimate pride that their children were semi-finalists in kabaddi and kho-kho state-level competitions. Overall, there was a greatly enhanced passion for participating in sports.

It was gratifying to hear the recently retired principal of the school, who had led the relationship with TMF over the last few years, sum up the results of the partnership in one sentence, 'TMF has dramatically upgraded our school.'

Swadhar

We spoke briefly about Swadhar in Chapter 3. Besides reading classes in municipal schools with the help of TMF, Swadhar endeavours to meet educational needs of slum children in other ways. Some of the children being served by Swadhar have an unusual background. Their fathers are camel drivers and, indeed, so are some of the boys themselves. Swadhar runs bridge courses for the children and then mainstreams them. It continues to give them remedial education to ensure they do not drop out. I met a group of fathers, who are camel drivers, and found them full of praise for what Swadhar had done for their children.

Swadhar's unique beneficiaries

These are not the only children Swadhar has helped. One of the many success stories is that of Baby Sheikh, who comes from a 'below poverty line' family that believed a girl child need not get any education. Swadhar teachers persuaded the family to let her join its classes and she went on to shine in high school. Armed with a scholarship thanks to her brilliant academic performance, she is now pursuing higher studies in the science stream. It was an absolute pleasure speaking to this cheerful, articulate young woman. Incidentally, she is one of the many Muslim girls and women in our various programmes whose self-confident personalities we may be unable to gauge simply because they are burqa clad!

Kagad Kach Patra Kashtkari Panchayat (KKPKP)

KKPKP is a union of waste pickers with 6,500 members. The credit for bringing it into existence goes to the Department of Continuing and Adult Education and Extension Work (Pune sub-centre) of SNDT Women's University, the well-known Mumbai-based institution. It is their flagship social outreach programme in Pune.

The work of KKPKP has brought about an amazing transformation in the lives and attitudes of members. Its process has instilled in the waste pickers a sense of self-esteem and the ability to collectively persuade the Pune municipal corporation to recognize them as important self-employed members of the informal sector of the economy with a valuable role in recycling scarce resources. This is remarkable considering their socio-economic background. However, SNDT/KKPKP believe that the next generation needs to have access to better livelihood opportunities. And, more urgently, it wishes to ensure that these children do not become child labourers joining their parents at work. Education was the obvious answer. And this is what provided scope for partnership between TMF and this unique association.

To ensure a well-structured approach to the problem of education of these children, one of the first activities undertaken with TMF funding was an extensive survey organized by SNDT on the number of children engaged in waste picking in different locations in Pune.

An immediate task was to raise overall awareness about education in the community. Over the years, this task has been successfully accomplished with very few KKPKP children now not enrolled in school. The next task was to ensure that the children remained in school. Earlier, there was large scale dropouts long before finishing school. To reverse this trend, TMF assisted KKPKP in carrying out several measures. Today, a majority of children go on to finish their schooling and very many advance onwards to college or vocational training courses.

TMF's assistance to KKPKP members and their children has taken different forms. For instance, the recurring cost of notebooks has always been a burden for poor parents. One of the first activities undertaken to help children's education was distribution of notebooks. In total, support was given to 2250 children of 1034 waste picker members across ninety-four slums of Pune and Pimpri Chinchwad municipal corporations. As was pointed out to us, this is not without a touch of irony as the waste pickers are instrumental in collecting many tonnes of paper for recycling each day!

Many scholarship programmes were instituted, including interest free loans for higher education. I witnessed an impressive felicitation programme where scholarships were distributed in the presence of children's caregivers. Students were given cash prizes for excelling in academics right from first standard till the SSC, HSC and graduation examinations. Cash prizes were also distributed to some girls who had been enrolled by their mothers or fathers four-five years ago for keeping their promise that they will study up to SSC level and not get married till eighteen.

In the same programme, an oath was taken publicly by all members to educate their children against all odds, not get any girl married before she reaches the legal age of marriage, ensure that all young children of waste pickers would be sent to the balwadis and also that they would never send their children for rag picking.

Sitting one evening in a meeting with the waste picker mothers, it was such joy to hear them encourage their daughters aspiring to be computer engineers, doctors, nurses, chartered accountants or even join the police force. When I went to some houses deep in the slums, there was enough evidence to show that these children were willing to work to achieve their dreams. A girl concentrating on her homework in the midst of blaring music and raucous squabbles of thoughtless neighbours, said simply, 'We have to get used to all this.'

While TMF does not specifically single out Dalit-targeted programmes when looking for partners, a very large number of the underprivileged inevitably belong to either the Scheduled Castes or Scheduled Tribes. In the case of KKPKP, it would be surprising if most did not belong to the Dalit community. This came through rather vividly when a bright brother-sister duo, were asked if they read anything besides textbooks, readily replied that they read books on Buddhism and the works of Babasaheb Ambedkar. They liked the thought of Buddha because he taught equality, fraternity and a philosophy of live and let live. They followed Ambedkar because he encouraged them to be self-reliant, helped break ancient oppressive customs and promoted 'bahujan samaj'. They have been brought up by their grandmother and an aunt, both waste pickers and members of KKPKP. Now in college, the brother aspires to be a computer engineer while the sister wants to teach.

Transformation: from the rag-picking grandmother to the college-going granddaughter

Sarvesham Seva Sangh

The husband–wife team of Prof. Usha and Vikas Wagh lead Sarvesham Seva Sangh which manages Samata Shikshan Sanstha. This is yet another NGO introduced to us by the earlier TMF team. A morning spent with the Wagh couple reveals their deep study of the problems faced by the children of Dalits, nomadic or ex-criminal tribes and commercial sex workers. For more than thirty years, their organization has provided a safe and cheerful environment for the education and overall development of these children.

It is easy to forget when you meet these children in the appropriately named Anand Ashram school and hostel run by this NGO that many have traumatic backgrounds. Some were orphaned at a very young age, many others have struggling single mothers.TMF has been happy to contribute to the needs of this institution, ranging from funding educational materials and supplying used computers for the computer lab to funding fun-packed vacation camps for children who have no home to go to during holidays. With the help of TMF, the school has organized facilities such as a soft skills programme, including spoken English. According to our Pune team, Vidya and Vijay effective use has been made of the TLMs bought with TMF funds. Their ability to read Marathi texts as well as perform in mathematics and science at their grade level are most encouraging.

Given the emotional needs of these children, TMF agreed to fund the appointment of a trained counsellor. Once again, according to Vijay's report, the counsellor, a young and enthusiastic person, has been able to extend valuable emotional support to many children.

'Our traumatic childhood is behind us'

The Sarvesham Seva Sangh has adopted the goal of achieving self-sufficiency as far as possible with respect to energy and food. It has harnessed solar and wind energy. Biogas has been generated by harnessing human waste. The vegetables at the simple but nutritious lunch which I enjoyed with them came from their own garden. Solar cooker and biogas had been used for cooking the food. The work with solar and wind energy, biogas, gardening and sericulture provides an opportunity for practical science experiments and for teaching important principle of sustainable development.

It was a pleasure to meet former students of this school who can now look forward to a life of dignity and self-reliance thanks to the care and education given them by TMF-assisted Samata Shikshan Sanstha. The sparkling smile of eighteen-year-old Meena proved how the loving environment has erased the sorrows of an orphaned childhood, and given her confidence to realize her dream of working for physically challenged children. Rupali, who came to the institution when she was nine, is a confident twenty-year-old and training to be an electronics engineer. Truly memorable was the meeting with Bhageshwari whose maturity and sense of responsibility belied the fact that she is barely out of her teens. Most of her friends have got married but she was determined 'to become something'. Her father died when she was very young and her mother ekes out a living as a vegetable vendor. Listening to her recite a poem written by her on a mother's love, her eyes filled with tears, was a deeply moving experience.

This simple statement by a girl, told to Vijay, says it all, 'I cannot go back home, I don't have one, school itself is home for me.'

India Sponsorship Committee (ISC)

ISC is yet another partner that has devoted itself to educating children in most difficult and vulnerable circumstances. It has taken up the challenge of bringing education to children from migrant families working in brick kilns in and around Pune and to wean them away from child labour. Many of these children are enrolled in their village schools but drop out of the educational system to join their parents at the brick kilns. The education of even those who do join schools gets badly disrupted when their parents move on to new working sites. As Vidya, our Pune-based manager, wrote, 'The children of brick kiln workers are among the most marginalized of all, growing up in sites with no electricity, sanitation or basic amenities, always under the spectre of being pulled into child labour to supplement the meagre family income.'

TMF supports eighteen ISC-run educational centres through which they cover around 500 children across thirty to thirty-five kilns located in the project area of ISC, about five kilometres away from Tech Mahindra's Hinjewadi location.

Some fun and games

During the five years of our partnership with ISC, we witnessed several encouraging changes. Other than the little ones who are in ISC-run balwadis, the children are mainstreamed in neighbouring schools but continue to enjoy strong remedial support by ISC. By the year 2010–11, every child from the project area, was enrolled in either a balwadi, a support class or a bridge class conducted by ISC. It was pleasing to hear about the girls who go to school travelling considerable distances on cycles presented by TMF.

Speaking to their parents, one found that many are now so convinced about the importance of education of their children that they have decided to abandon their earlier peripatetic life style and look for livelihood opportunities in the neighbourhood when there is no work in the brick kilns.

On each of my field visits, I was impressed by the professionalism of the ISC workers. Some of them have forged a remarkable level of rapport with the schools to which these children go. One of the mothers told me about how her eight-year-old son was refusing to go to school because of corporal punishment by his teacher. Saira Sheikh of ISC went and met the teacher. Result: the teacher stopped beating the child who resumed his schooling.

In fact, I had more than one occasion to be awed by Saira's dedication. One year, my field visit coincided with month of Ramzan. There was torrential rain that day and the path—there was no road—to the ISC classes slushy and full of muck. But there was Saira, who had walked a long distance—I have forgotten precisely how long but I remember being struck at that time by the distance this fasting girl had covered—happily settled with her students who clearly adored her.

A very committed Saira

> **Saira's Story:**
>
> I used to be a housewife like most of the women in my community; wearing a burqa until the time when I started teaching the children in the brick kilns of Maan, which is run by the India Sponsorship Committee. This is where I experienced real freedom.
>
> I began to see the importance of being a teacher. I realized that the position of a teacher was high and also that while imparting education to children, I was educating myself. My general knowledge improved and I learnt how to talk and present myself.
>
> My interest in my work increased and I began enjoying myself. I now feel a closeness with both the parents (brick kiln workers) and the children, and we cooperate with each other. I love the children and they too like me very much.
>
> Saira Shaikh

When meeting the parents—many of whom had never been to school themselves and are subjected to exploitation by the brick kiln owners—one once again experiences the joy of hearing them declare their commitment to children's education. Alas, in some cases a distinction was drawn between the son, who would be encouraged to study to as high a level as he could manage, and the daughter in whose case they would be satisfied to see her finish high school and then get her married. Obviously, it

'We shall educate our children'

will take some time before patriarchic norms change. But one thing is clear: be it boy or girl, the parents are determined that their children will have sufficient education to break through the poverty cycle and will not have to go through the same back-breaking asthma-producing work in the brick kilns as they did.

Elsewhere, I shall have occasion to speak in some detail about the volunteering by Tech Mahindra associates. But I can mention here that, taking advantage of the fact that ISC work sites are not very far from TM's Hinjewadi office, about a dozen TM volunteers would go and teach English every weekend, something much appreciated by their students.

Shashwat

To facilitate monitoring by the TMF staff and volunteering by Tech Mahindra associates, we have, as a general principle, chosen NGOs that work in cities where TMF is located. Only half a dozen or so of our partners work in rural settings; these are not merely exceptions but indeed exceptional. One of these is Shashwat, one of the very few working with tribal communities.

Shashwat is the creation of the extraordinary husband-wife team of Anand Kapoor and Kusum Karnik. Anand graduated from IIT Kharagpur in the mid-1970s. His life changed when he met Kusum, a social activist. The couple was deeply troubled by the poverty, humiliation and exploitation to which tribals were subjected to. Leading modest Gandhian lives, they have built an organization with a holistic approach that includes education, livelihood and ardent advocacy of tribal rights. Profound respect is shown by them and their team for the distinct culture of these nomadic tribals.

For five years, TMF supported the Vandeo Vidya Mandir Residential Primary school they run in Aghane village in Ambegaon Taluka of the Pune District for sixty children of Katkari tribals. The children who graduate from this school are encouraged to join the secondary school some distance away in Dimbhe. A hostel set up for them was also supported partially by TMF.

Anand Kapoor

Kusum Karnik

The school was started in 2001 to cater to the needs of tribal children, especially girls, who are unable to cope with the regular primary school systems in the tribal area of Ambegaon block. The organization is sparing no effort towards making Vandeo Vidya Mandir school a model primary school for tribal education in the area where it is located. Tribals of the Mahadeo Koli and Thakar tribes and the Katkari primitive tribe live in this remote, difficult to access area in the steeply sloping, heavily forested area of the Western Ghats which gets heavy rainfall.

The primary school has overcome many of the challenges presented by its sheer remoteness. It cannot be easy to get qualified teachers to come and teach in this school. Teachers of the school go through various training programmes on a regular basis. As a result, government inspectors who have conducted detailed evaluation have been quite satisfied by the quality of learning in the school.

The school opens a new world for these tribal children

Though the brief visits—one by me and several by our Pune-based team—may not enable us to get an in-depth understanding of the life and education of these children, one does get the impression of a well-run school.

In contrast to what is known about the poverty and malnutrition in this community, the children of this school seem to be in good health and reasonably well fed. It was pleasing to learn of the great opportunity the children get to take part in sports. What we were able to see during our brief visit was a very impressive display of a traditional lezim dance performance.

The background of the children reflects itself in the arts and the crafts they make of local materials available to them: model agricultural implements, for instance, crafted from wood and mud. Also, they make models and charts explaining the seasons, night and day, sketches of old-style musical instruments, windmills, and even the Great Wall of China!

Speaking to the older children who have moved to the hostel, one gets the impression that they have integrated reasonably well with fellow non-tribal students. They did sing, for my benefit, in a rousing chorus, a song asserting tribal rights to 'jungle and zameen'. One hopes these first generation learners will later in life make use of the empowerment conferred on them by education to help their own community in its struggle to lead a life of dignity and well-being. The challenge obviously is to retain their distinct cultural identity while confidently meeting the demands of modernity. In the meantime, not surprisingly, the aspirations of most of these teenagers are like those of any other young persons:

From Shashwat

Tech Mahindra Foundation (TMF) was the first Indian corporate donor to support for six long years (2006–13) our efforts to provide an opportunity to access education for tribal & primitive tribe children—those who never went to school or couldn't adjust to the existing system of Tribal Development Dept Ashram schools or Zilla Parishad schools, children living in the most remote hilly tribal area of Pune district.

onwards march to a college education in the nearby town followed by a successful working career in some urban setting.

One of the most exciting outings for the Vandeo school children was to the Tech Mahindra office in Pune. Full credit to our Pune executives for organizing this event. The children felt truly welcomed. Walking through the office was an eye-opener for them. It was also a learning experience for TM staff many of whom, led by senior most officials like C.P. Gurnani, came out to meet and talk to the children. During the trip, the children also visited the IUCAA Science Centre, a wonderful place designed to popularize science with many opportunities for children to play with scientific gadgets.

TMF officers were friendly with children and acted with trust with our organization, though they were keenly observant and took proper care to gauge the quality of our work. They supported our 4-year program to provide special maths education program to Std 1–4, which led children to lose their fear of math and for teachers to become confident in math teaching. TMF introduced our children to science education with toys through Mr Arvind Gupta and the team of IUCAA Pune. They carefully checked our accounts and appreciated our efforts at maintaining transparency.

TMF took care to support our efforts for children's welfare, whether it was for making masonry steps to go down to the well and enough toilets, or for purchase of sufficient warm clothes and blankets for the children. They supported our efforts to promote sports, extra-curricular activities and exposure visits for the tribal children; they also supported our efforts to provide hostel facility with educational coaching for these kids after passing 4th std., in another nearby school so that they may not drop out again.

TMF also provided special opportunities for SHASHWAT personnel in computer education and involvement with other CSR programs in Pune district. Our people were always respectfully treated by TMF officers and their manner was always friendly and supportive to all of us.

Thank you TMF with all our heart and let us be in touch in future also.

With best wishes and regards,

Yours sincerely,
For SHASHWAT

Kusum Karnik, Vice President & Co-Founder
Anand Kapoor, Project Coordinator
Budhaji Damse, School Manager
Pratibha Tambe, Managing Trustee

Indian Institute of Education (IIE)

IIE is the brain child of one of independent India's

best known educationists, the late J.P. Naik. The institute has undertaken several research projects on behalf of the government relating to the education of the marginalized. The proposal they submitted to us dealt with an important national problem highlighted by the Sachar committee: an action research project on the failure of the Muslim community to take full advantage of educational opportunities. As IIE pointed out in its proposal, progress is not uniform amongst religious groups and some minority groups are distinctly lagging behind. Of 1000 Muslim women in urban areas, 445 are illiterate as compared with 306 Hindu and 122 Christian; only 34 Muslim women have reached graduation as compared to 109 Hindu women and 150 Christian.

In order to understand the phenomenon in a proper perspective, and find out the root causes of the problem, IIE has concentrated on education amongst Muslims as a priority area. A series of projects were undertaken to study the education of Muslim girls in Pune municipal schools right at the entry level i.e. primary education. Their preliminary studies having confirmed that the dropout rates of girls are high, IIE submitted to us a three-year action research project entitled 'Intervention for preventing school drop out of the children from the minority community with focus on Pune municipal schools'. It pointed out the need to create a model that would be essentially participative in nature and involve all stakeholders such as parents, teachers, community leaders, government officials and students. It would include many action programmes like the opening of Khel Ghars, or play groups, teacher trainings and parent-teacher meetings and create an environment to generate interest amongst children and result in reduced dropouts.

IIE interacts with parents

The action research project would also investigate whether the municipal schools in the area accurately reflected the demographic diversity of the local population. It selected three municipal schools in economically backward areas in Pune with substantial Muslim population for action research on the issue. Built into the proposal was a plan to prevent children from the minority community dropping out of school. Underlying the project was also the thought that ensuring inclusion of minority students in the mainstream educational system should not mean communal segregation at the level of school education, which could be the foundation of misunderstandings between the two communities. The importance of the issue being addressed by the proposed project was obvious.

The project was headed by Dr Razia Patel. She is a well-known authority on the subject.

The programme is aimed at improvements in formal educational aspects as well as non-formal education, which will create the interest of the children in overall education and, importantly, includes development of scientific values with the help of games.

When I visited one of these schools, the research project had just begun but it was clear that IIE's presence had made this school more attractive. The presence of IIE's two social workers, workshops for parents and teachers and the Khel Ghar for the children had made sure that there would be no more dropouts. The hope is that these various creative interventions, which were practical being low cost, would be replicated in other municipal schools.

> I had an opportunity to work with TMF since last 3 years, while working on a project at Indian Institute of Education, regarding inclusive education of minorities at Pune, and I consider it as a very valuable and unique experience. The issues regarding Muslim backwardness are very complex, both from economic perspective, and from minority perspective. We had come across very few institutions supporting CSR on this subject, owing to the misunderstandings about this community and Hindu–Muslim relations. It should be recognized that Muslims are second largest community in India, and if this community remains backward in education it essentially affects the progress of entire nation. However, TMF was a pleasant surprise in this regard, and it demonstrated very responsible thinking while supporting the project wholeheartedly with commitment . . . As a result the project is coming out with very unique and valuable findings about importance of holistic approach and community participation in improving municipal education for Muslim children.
>
> Razia

Action for the Rights of Children

The Foundation has also been associated with the Pune-based Action for the Rights of Children (ARC), a forum which seeks to bring together organizations working for the rights, including the right to education (RTE), of the poorest children of Pune. In 2009, some leading ARC members approached us saying that the network was greatly handicapped by the lack of a full-time coordinator. We have met this modest need and have been admiring witnesses to the tremendous work ARC is doing. Naturally, the collective voice of twenty-plus NGOs—many that are or were our partners—makes a persuasive impact on the Pune Municipal Corporation (PMC) and various government departments. Particularly impressive is the work they are doing now to ensure that the RTE act is implemented in its true spirit. Earlier, they succeeded in persuading the PMC to make effective arrangements for the schooling of migrant labour. They have unitedly struggled against child labour and such child-related issues as corporal punishment.

7

Educational Initiatives in the National Capital Region

Vidya and Child

Not too far from the Noida Golf Course is a slum community named after the father of our Constitution, B.R. Ambedkar. Within that is the Harijan basti where the largest of the four centres run by our partner Vidya and Child (V&C) is located. Managed by the Jayaprakash Narayan Memorial Trust, its lead figure is Supriya Akhoury, the grand niece of the famous Loknayak. We have already mentioned this organization in Chapter 5 as the one helping us with the concept of Lab School running in tandem with In Service Education Institute. There was a very good reason why we selected Vidya and Child for that pioneering task. It is due to the immensely encouraging experience we have had with its main educational programme for vulnerable children.

V&C provides a very well organized education programme from nursery to class five for over a 1000 children whose parents are rickshaw drivers, fruit and vegetable vendors and domestic maids. The organization also runs a highly effective after-school support programme for children mainstreamed to other schools from sixth standard onwards, once they have acquired a strong foundation. Indeed, V&C has gradually taken over the responsibility for the entire education life cycle of its children, all the way up to their finding a meaningful career.

V&C had already been working for seven years when our partnership began on a small scale in 2007. We responded positively to their request to fund their content design project. As explained by the group, this grant led to the development of content in the form of a teachers manual and workbooks for all classes from nursery to fourth standard for English, Hindi, maths, science, etc.:

- The teachers' manual is a guide to enable teachers to teach each topic using different methods and activities so that she can ensure that each child learns.
- It is used as a base for training conducted internally for all teachers to strengthen their teaching skills.
- The workbooks provide adequate practice and reinforcement opportunities in the form of worksheets.

The content has helped create a class environment, rich in learning materials, that enables children to use their inherent capacity to learn. The content today is used by over fifty teachers to teach over 1000 learners across four communities in Noida where V&C has centres. In subsequent years, we were happy to see the excellent result of this project on the learning levels of children.

TMF went on to support the Harijan basti centre for the next five years. This continuous support has helped V&C, to quote its report, 'to consolidate, work on quality, keep identifying gaps and keep increasing outreach every year'.

TMF was so impressed by the quality of education provided by V&C that besides supporting other elements of their work, in a rare exception, we gave them funds for building a new centre in Noida (village Barola) for which another donor had gifted the land.

Supriya briefs teachers in the Barola centre while little ones marvel at the new world of computers

V&C children not only get a strong academic grounding but also a wide range of extracurricular opportunities. Particularly outstanding is the Arts & Performing Arts Programme (A&PA) designed 'for exploring the unique potential within each child' where each child can choose from among a variety of performing arts: kathak, tabla, theatre, music and even filmmaking.

More than once have their girls regaled audiences at our Shikshak Samman award functions with their kathak performances. Many of their boys have acquired impressive competence in playing tabla.

In February 2012, we were privileged to see V&C children showcase their creative skills in such fields as robotics, filmmaking and editing and western dance at India International Centre. This was one of the many projects the group does for its children in collaboration with volunteers from other organizations, in this case, Dreaming Child Productions and Atelier Theatre Group. I was not surprised to learn that a film on water conservation made by the children of V&C won the first prize in the Little Director's category of the International Children's Film Festival 2011.

I spent a humbling afternoon with some children whose lives have been transformed by the synergy between V&C's

Vidya and Child girls at TMF's SSA awards

Deepika and her mother: one more dream coming true

endeavours and their own willpower. Nineteen-year-old Deepika, who was earlier compelled by family's economic circumstances to work as a domestic servant, was brought into education by Supriya. Having done her tenth through open schooling, she obtained a full-time marketing job. This was cut short by a scooter accident. Once again encouraged by Supriya, Deepika resumed her studies and passed her twelfth. She is currently working in McDonald's and simultaneously doing a Bachelor's in Business Administration and is determined to find a more challenging job. In the meanwhile, her earnings enable her siblings to go to normal schools. Like many other mothers I met in the course of writing this book, her mother too strongly backs her career aspirations and is not rushing her into an early marriage. Expressing her gratitude for what V&C has done for her, Deepika speaks of the emotional handholding by Supriya and her team, helping her in moments of despair, encouraging her to overcome apprehension of failure.

The next V&C alumna I met was Sunita, who joined the organization when she was seven and now, ten years later, is studying in one of Noida's top schools on the strength of a scholarship. This brilliant student is preparing, with V&C's help, for the Joint Engineering Entrance examination. Looking back at her years with V&C, she is grateful to it not only for giving her a good education, including kathak, but also because it taught her *'khud ko pehchanna'* (understanding oneself).

Another V&C 'graduate' who has won a scholarship to an elite school is sixteen-year-old Devi Shankar. His dream is to enter the National Defence Academy and one day become an infantry officer in the army. Devi also happens to be an accomplished tabla player.

Supriya explains the value of music and dance for her children. 'It dissolves the negatives which many of these children have to confront at home: domestic violence, alcoholism and other poverty-generated problems.'

Bharat Ratna Jayaprakash Narayan would certainly be proud of the service rendered to the poor by his very modest, soft-spoken and highly dedicated grand niece.

Katha

The contribution of Delhi-based NGO Katha in the field of literature is well known. But it has also done remarkable work in the field of education for the underprivileged. We have already spoken of Katha in Chapter 3 where we surveyed the work done by TMF in improving the quality of education in municipal schools.

But TMF's partnership with this remarkable organization led by Padma Shri Geeta Dharmarajan commenced with support to the school run by it for the economically challenged children of Govindpuri slum cluster, which they rightly call the Katha Lab School. It has many innovative features and it serves as some sort of a resource of quality education for government and municipal schools.

Referring to the partnership with TMF, Katha's website says:

'With their [TMF's] steady support and cooperation, the Katha Lab School has emerged as the centre of creative education, reaching out to lakhs of children in the slums, streets, government and municipal schools of Delhi and Haryana and tribal areas of Arunachal Pradesh. The Katha Lab School has proved to be a powerful tool for enabling children and youths to reach their highest potential, and the results have been overwhelmingly positive!'

Govindpuri shares the usual characteristics of most Delhi slums: small, dingy, poorly ventilated single room accommodations in the narrowest possible lanes lined with open drains, but with a vibrant life of its own.

One of the distinctive features of Katha's approach that attracted us was the manner in which it embedded 'community revitalization' in its curriculum. Located right in the midst

Govindpuri: the setting of Katha Lab School

of the sprawling slum, the school has consistently sought to relate its educational projects to the realities and needs of this neighbouring habitation.

On one of my first visits to the Katha school many years ago, I was struck by the sight of boys and girls working with great concentration and excitement on a project with the help of their computer teachers to determine the level of purity—or, more accurately, the impurity—of the drinking water available in their colony. I later learnt of the door-to-door health survey conducted by the children; these results were then fed into their computers for analysis.

This and similar other projects are then leveraged to bring about improvements in the life of their community. Thus, for instance, a maths exercise was linked to determining the daily per capita availability of water. It was established that this was a mere quarter of a bucket. The findings were converted into a power point presentation before the Chief Minister.

'We know the value of computers'

Similarly, letter writing skills acquired in the classroom are used to write letters for the community to various departments.

It comes as no surprise to see how well some former Katha students are doing in life. They look back with a deep sense of gratitude at what Katha did for them both inside and outside the classroom. The loving care of teachers is recalled with barely concealed emotion. I met this alumna of Katha who has gone on to do a MA in political science and is now working at a call centre while determinedly preparing to appear in public service examinations . . . an aspiring IAS officer. I was also moved after meeting with another young alumnus, who went on to get an engineering degree and now holds a responsible job in Delhi Metro. It is a measure of the transformation brought about Katha in the fortunes of a family over a single generation that both his parents did not have the good fortune to go to school.

geeta dharmarajan

katha | new delhi | india
tel: +91.11.26.52.17.52 | www.katha.org

follow us on twitter: http://twitter.com/KathaIndia
follow us on facebook: http://www.facebook.com/kathaindia

'Never doubt that a small group of thoughtful committed citizens can change the world, indeed it is the only thing that ever has.' Margaret Mead
How do we count the ways that the partnership with Tech Mahindra Foundation from the very start has helped our children, women and communities to achieve their potential. What words would suffice to describe the genuine warmth and friendship we received from the beginning of our partnership. Since Day One, TMF leadership and team members understood the urgency and need to scale up our work in quality ways, so that more and more children could benefit. And always, with them, it was mutual respect and attempt to find a solution for the challenges that faced our children, their families. I remember so well the very first visits that Vinod Khannaji made to our school. He would sit with our School of Entrepreneurship students, helping them to sort out issues they faced as they prepared to move into the real world. Every visit was a mini workshop of immense value. And then we were blessed with Loveleen Kackerji's warm-hearted, spontaneous support.

The most exciting current activity is Katha going digital with TMF's help. The next year promises to be full of innovative energy! Katha's committed staff and our fun loving children and community women join me in saying: Thank you people of TMF who made and make it one of the most generous and amazing organisation Katha has had.

Katha has been very conscious of the fact that its children may have talents that go beyond academic ability and would help them pursue fulfilling careers in life. In fact, the perfect match between a teacher's lifelong passion for athletics and a student's talent defines one heartwarming story. As a schoolgirl, the teacher, Shabana, was an outstanding athlete herself but, as she grew older, she ran into determined opposition from her conservative Muslim family. So, instead, Shabana now encourages athletics in her school and speaks proudly of all the medals her students have won. Most striking is the story of Pushpendra Pande, who like Shabana is a superb runner. But he comes from a very poor family—his father is a plumber and mother a housewife. Unable to afford even the most basic equipment, he began by running barefoot. But, encouraged by the school, he went on to win gold medals for his age group in events like 800m, 1500m and long jump. Soon, professional coaches took him on and he was also able to get sponsors. Unfortunately, a back injury has interrupted his athletic career but he remains in the field, doing a course to secure a bachelor's degree in physical education and plans to go on to take

Pushpendra and his atheletics guru Shabana

a master's degree. In the meanwhile, he works for Magic Bus, an NGO supported by TMF, which forges an alliance between sports and education. Pushpendra reveals shyly that he plays a small role in the film on the hero of every Indian aspiring athlete, Milkha Singh.

Shikhar

An NGO named Shikhar approached us with a request to support a condensed course which it runs in Okhla for some 350 girls who had had to abandon their schooling prematurely but now willing to complete their schooling as a stepping stone to a more fruitful life. Classes nine to twelve are run along standard lines. The teaching methodology is not particularly innovative but it is adequate to ensure that all the girls—the overwhelming majority of whom are Muslims—are able to finish schooling and then go on to do what was previously unthinkable for them: join college or get decent jobs.

I was struck each time I visited the 'school' by the commitment of these young women, a very visible determination to start a new life.

Batla House in Okhla sometimes appears in the news for the wrong reasons. But on a normal day, the experience of walking through its narrow lanes and meeting the people who live and work there is no different from visiting any of urban India's thousands of low-income colonies. Among those living here is Khalida, one more girl determined to break the shackles of poverty by completing her education. She was a bright student but had to abandon her education early when her father fell mortally ill and the entire family fortune was consumed in his treatment. Persuaded by Shikhar she is back, has finished her twelfth and is about to enter college. It was profoundly moving to meet her and her brave mother who is willing to forego the

Higher education: a key to empowerment

income Khalida was earning so she can move ahead and build a better future for herself.

What is fascinating about the Shikhar programme is that it goes well beyond the classroom. It opens a whole new world for these girls miles away from their otherwise rather cloistered lives: self-defence courses, sports, participation in TV programmes, meeting inspirational figures, painting in summer camps and so on. The organization is greatly helped by its proximity to Jamia Milia Islamia whose facilities they are able to use. It is also able to draw upon resource persons from Jamia to speak to the girls on issues relating to health, hygiene and legal rights.

Witnessing their cultural programmes, held in one or the other of the auditoriums of Jamia Milia is a delightful experience. The exuberance and sheer joy with which the girls sing, dance and act is in dramatic contrast to the economic and social challenges they face in their daily lives. Item after item in these lively afternoons is imbued with the spirit of India's cultural pluralism.

Khalida and mother: a new approach to life

Social Outreach Foundation

Naturally, we have been specially keen to support groups working with marginalized children in areas close to our offices where possible. The Social Outreach Foundation (SOF) in Noida is one such organization. SOF was established by the alumnae of the Isabella Thoburn College, Lucknow. It runs a good quality primary school in Sector 37 of Noida for children from very poor families. In many cases, fathers do not have steady incomes as vegetable vendors and rickshaw pullers and mothers are overworked as domestic helpers.

SOF has a deep commitment to the children's future and so the organization also sponsors the brighter of its 'graduates' to neighbouring public schools. At the request of SOF, strongly supported by our executive Shashi, TMF has been supporting this post primary support project, which includes financial aid for regular schooling, participation in extracurricular activities, additional tuitions and counselling support for personality and communication development. If these children are not supported beyond the primary level, there is danger of their having to drop out from the educational stream and becoming child labourers.

Some of the children who have been mentored by SOF have gone on to very fulfilling careers. At a recent annual day celebration, one of their former students greatly moved the audience when he spoke of his journey from an exceedingly poor childhood to a successful career as a choreographer, thanking SOF and his mother who was present. Another student, a smart young woman, told me about her preparations to become an air hostess.

Magic Bus India Foundation

We all know from our own experience how important a role sports played in our school education. The well-known Magic Bus Foundation, a relatively new partner, works towards development of personality of economically underprivileged children through sports.

Nikhil Pant, who was then a senior executive in TMF, visited some Magic Bus centres in Mumbai and reported that it was a very well structured programme and quite a unique one too. The sessions are conducted very professionally with a lot of seriousness from both the trainers and the children. He observed that Magic Bus is well focused on the impact analysis of its programmes.

I followed this up with a visit to one of its programmes in Delhi and was struck by the simple yet imaginative ways in which Magic Bus weaves into sports precisely the objectives which we hope for in the playing field. The youth are empowered to assume leadership roles. Harmonious teamwork is promoted. Excellence combined with fair play is encouraged. And boys and girls find themselves adapting to a concept quite foreign in their daily lives: gender equality.

We must confess that at least in one school the programme failed to take off. A misunderstanding between a Magic Bus worker and some students led to an unfortunate incident and the programme had to be pulled out from that school. But elsewhere it appears to have been a most welcome addition to the educational programmes being run by some of our NGO partners. As we noted in Chapter 5, Magic Bus is an integral part of our 'ARISE' exercise in the Kasturba Balika Vidyalaya.

8

Educational Initiatives in Mumbai

Besides the very important work our NGO partners are doing with municipal schools in Mumbai of which we spoke in Chapter 3, we have had the good fortune of being associated with a few other excellent educational programmes, some of which are completely unrelated to government educational system and others only partially so.

Learning to Lead

TMF has been constantly on the lookout for programmes beyond the classroom and textbooks that enrich the educational experience of children from economically poor background. Many of these programmes are experimental in nature with few donors willing to take the risk of supporting them for fear of not being able to see a visible impact.

One programme TMF decided to support when—according to the NGO—hardly any other donor seemed interested was Akanksha Foundation's Learning to Lead (LTL) programme. LTL sought to identify children from Akanksha classes and government-aided schools (students from a low economic strata) with the potential and motivation for leadership and academic excellence. They are selected on the basis of their general and academic performances, IQ levels and their family backgrounds. One reason why other donors may have hesitated was the relatively high per-child cost of this unique venture, besides the difficulty to measure outcomes.

At LTL, there is focus on two streams—leadership and academics. The leadership curriculum, which includes language, leadership studies and literature, ensures critical and reflective thinking. On the academic side, support is provided to the students for all formal school subjects. Students are encouraged to take part in extracurricular activities at school or at Akanksha. The students are also counselled to deal with interpersonal issues, study skills and stress management. A sense of social responsibility is instilled in them.

Ashwini: 'Thanks to Akanksha and TMF, I dream of becoming a doctor'

We shared Akanksha's belief in these children, some of whom come from typical slums, full of human misery and physical filth. But they have demonstrated amazing resilience and determination. There is for instance this brilliant girl, Ashwini, who got 89 per cent in SSC and is growing up in a dingy jhuggi in a terribly crowded and noisy neighbourhood. She dreams of being a doctor one day but is realistic enough to have a backup plan to be a paramedic. In the meanwhile, she combines her studies with teaching younger children.

I asked an LTL boy about how this programme made him different from his classmates. Prompt came the reply, 'I learnt to think for myself, to be rational, to look for causes and not to follow the herd blindly.'

Not all the LTL children came from slums but all came from economically disadvantaged families. One such brilliant girl is Shubangi Nagaria, who scored 93 per cent in the CBSE examination. Her father works as a water supplier with the Military Engineering Services and the family lives in modest official quarters. She is a first generation learner who now aspires to become an IAS officer. This is how she herself describes her journey with LTL:

Five years ago, I was selected for the LTL programme after a rigorous selection process. At that time, I was in 7th grade and I was unsure about joining as the programme seemed demanding. My mother and sister, who was part of the programme, had to push me a lot to join the programme. Learning to Lead was a 3 hour after-school programme. It was frustrating to go after school while all my friends were hanging out and playing. Didis kept on motivating me and put a lot of emphasis on teaching us leadership values.

Now when I look back in time, I am glad I took the path less travelled and joined LTL. I have realized that it was worth it.

At LTL, reading, writing, leadership case studies and fun activities all happened simultaneously which made it interesting. With every book I read, my curiosity for reading another book increased. Various projects, presentations and events boosted my confidence. I am no more an introvert and interact with people without hesitation.

We went for leadership retreats where we were exposed to inspiring organizations, corporate, educational institutes and leaders. I felt privileged to visit corporate giants such as Infosys, Tech Mahindra and Google and premier educational institutes such as Symbiosis, and Welham Girls School. I also visited SIDH (Society for Integrated Development of Himalayas) which has changed my definition of education. Education is not just about books, but it's about knowledge along with experience.

I have developed research, analytical and critical thinking skills and inculcated values such as high expectations, being the change, perseverance and humility. In addition, I have learnt how to overcome obstacles and make right choices. After all a bend in the road is not the end of it unless you choose to take a turn.

I wish I live up to my expectations and make my parents proud. I truly believe in the quote by Robert Frost, 'Two roads diverged in a yellow wood and I chose the road less travelled by.' That's how I want to make a difference in my life and to people around me. It is my journey towards 'Being the Change', becoming financially independent and also being a role model.

> I have seen Learning to Lead morph from a concept to a full fledged leadership and academic achievement programme. Today, LTL students have graduated with degrees in B.Sc, B.Com and B.A., pursuing M.Sc. in genetics, M.Com., Master's in H.R, Bachelors in Fine Arts. There are students who have scored distinction in Board exams including 93% in CBSE. They have had exposure beyond academics to sports, drama, dance, inspiring leaders and organizations. From taking leadership initiatives in college to leading events in Akanksha, from teaching maths at Akanksha centres to making presentations to colleges and corporates.
>
> LTL has been supported by TMF since 2007. It is this support that had helped LTL reach out to more children and achieve its objectives. Partnership with TMF has been more than a financial partnership. The TMF team has believed in the programme, its objectives, and seen the impact which has fed back into their belief system.
>
> TMF actively supported us by attending LTL's various events such as Community Research projects and Year-end programme and asked relevant and thought-provoking questions to the students. In addition, they would visit the Centre regularly, observe the classes, interact with the students.
>
> Poorvi Shah
> Akanksha
> Coordinator, LTL programme

Not all LTL products may be as outstanding as

Ashwini and Shubhangi but almost all are headed towards careers which would have been unthinkable without this imaginative Akanksha programme. There is the boy who is the son of gardener and a domestic maid who has appeared for the National Talent Search (NTS) exam and also cleared the entrance test for Vidyalankar Institute which prepares for IIT JEE. Another boy, whose family suffered a major setback when the father lost his job because the mill in which he worked closed down, is now interning with a chartered accountants firm. And these are typical of the life trajectories of these budding leaders.

I was somewhat disappointed when I learnt recently that Akanksha was winding down this programme. But I was assured that this was only to enable them to take the lessons learnt in running this to a larger set of children, in fact, to all the children in the various schools where they are working.

Children's Toy Foundation, Mumbai (CTF)

When our Mumbai-based executive Swati, who had just been recruited, spoke to me about the Children's Toy Foundation (CTF) I was rather dismissive. As she was convinced that its work genuinely enriched children's education, I agreed to meet Devendra Shivlal Desai, the founder and managing trustee of this NGO.

To meet Desai is an invitation to take a journey down memory lane, back to some of the most enjoyable and exciting moments of one's childhood. He seems to live, dream and think toys. But toys for him are not merely instruments for entertaining children. He has given deep thought to how, apart from being a source of enjoyment in itself, toys and games can also be instrumental in the physical, social, emotional and cognitive development of children in municipal schools even as they enjoy themselves. Not only does he subscribe passionately to the child's right to play, he believes that playing games impacts children in many ways. It enhances the decision making and problem solving skills of children, enhances their social skills and leads to peer-to-peer learning.

Desai has categorized games into logical, analytical, maths, creative, dice and puzzle categories. There are also games based on the curriculum. His team is trained to unobtrusively let the toys and games work their educational magic.

It was wonderful to see children enjoying themselves while working on complex puzzles or playing chess in the play centre which we support in one of the schools. Certainly, the children would like to spend more time than the one hour a week that their time table permits.

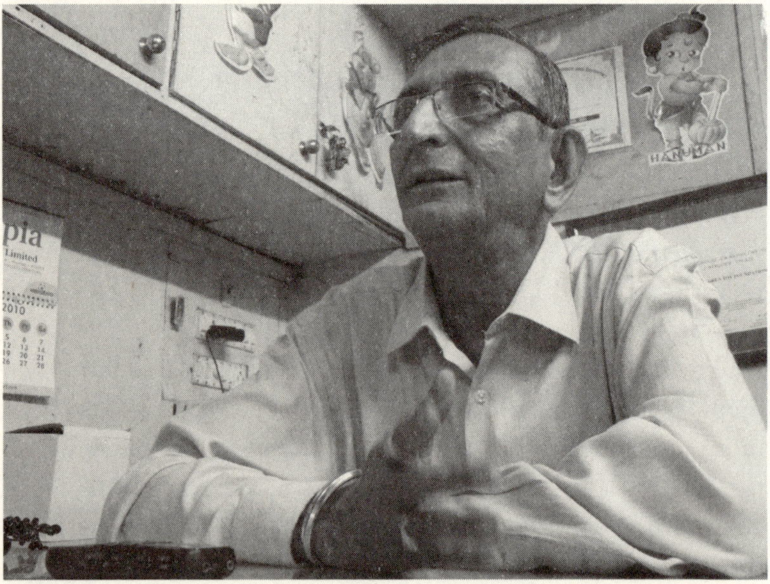

Devendra Shivlal Desai: 'I believe in educational potential of toys'

'We learn so much through toys and games'

CTF also has a few toy vans which enable it to reach out to several schools. TMF funds one of these vans. The majority of municipal schools lack any facility for extracurricular activities like the ones conducted by CTF, but opening up play centres in each of these schools is rather difficult due to the lack of space and high set up cost. This is where the van plays a very important role. It is used to carry toys and games to a school every day and conduct one hour sessions for classes one to four as per a fixed time table in each of the classes. The van is also used to conduct summer camps and conduct competitions during the holidays.

CTF is currently working in twenty-five vernacular medium municipal schools and ten schools of mobile creches in Mumbai. It was encouraging to learn from our Mumbai executive that CTF gets good support from municipal corporation officials.

Desai's passionate dedication to the cause so dear to him reflects in the help CTF renders to other organizations in setting up toy libraries. It has set up 280 such libraries so far but aspires to set up more across the country, especially in remote villages where the children do not have any access to toys and games.

Masoom

Led by Nikita Ketkar, a determined young lady who resigned from a comfortable government job to take up this challenge, Masoom seeks to transform a certain number of night schools in Mumbai. Most of these schools are at 'D' level (as per the government's evaluation tool) and Masoom is planning to upgrade these schools to 'A' level.

There are about 150 night schools in Mumbai but they have been neglected both by the government and non-government organizations. All night schools are run by private trusts with

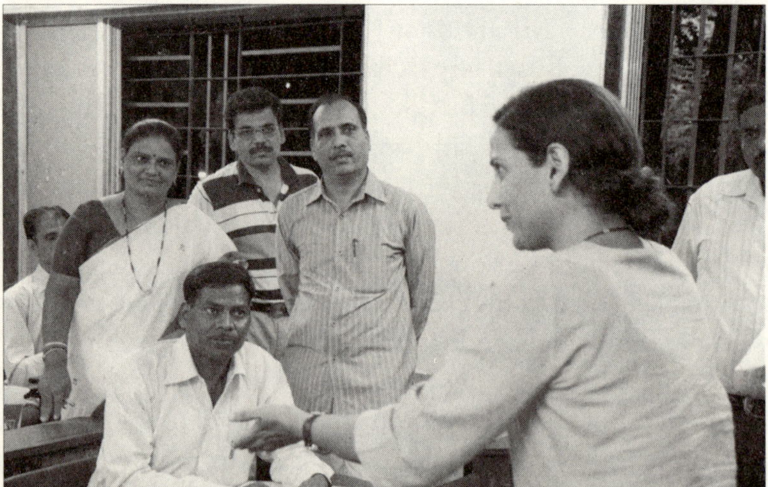

Nikita motivating the teachers

'We work during the day'

government funding restricted to salary grants. With limited financial support from the government and lack of funds with the trusts, the quality of education in night schools has been suffering for many years. Night schools face additional challenges. They run at night and remain invisible to society. They are attended by children and young people who work during the day and belong to poorer sections of society.

The students are not charged any fees. The teachers have to complete the curriculum with only three hours of teaching time every day. Many students have had a gap in their education. Hence, their level of knowledge is invariably far lower than the grade in which they are studying.

When our partnership began with Masoom, it was working with standards eighth, ninth and tenth in fifteen night schools and

My experience with Tech Mahindra has been unique. Our first meeting with all potential donors is very formal. We generally have a scheduled meeting with the donors which proceeds in a formal way. The experience with Tech Mahindra was different. Swati came to us and enquired about our programme and I first thought she was a volunteer and so was very comfortable talking to her about Masoom and the challenges we were facing. After a while I realized that she was representing Tech Mahindra.

I liked her approach and was impressed that she knew about night schools and the work that we are doing.

Generally our donor meetings happen in donors' offices or Masoom office. In these meetings we discuss the reporting formats and deliverables that Masoom will achieve, but with Tech Mahindra most of our meetings happened in the schools with the teachers and Head masters. Swati has an understanding of the programme and the challenges we face and that helped her to connect to our programme in schools.

Vidya's visits to our night schools have been very motivating for our students. Besides understanding the programme she has made it a point to speak to our students to motivate them.

We see Tech Mahindra as a partner who has come in to support Masoom in realizing its vision by taking the ownership of the programme. We see Tech Mahindra as not just a donor agency doling out grants but a partner who is aware of the ground realities and challenges and is willing to support Masoom in overcoming the challenges.

I would like to thank Tech Mahindra team for choosing Masoom. We are highly privileged to be a part of the Tech Mahindra family.

Nikita

planned to take up five more schools the following year. The classes are run from 7 p.m. to 10 p.m. About 30 per cent of the students are girls. Each school has around eighty students.

Masoom is working towards improving the quality of education by providing educational material, bridge classes, English speaking classes, science lab, teacher training, sports facility, library, counselling, nutrition etc. It also runs a career cell which helps the students to enrol for higher studies/vocational training or to find jobs.

Night schools clearly serve an important function. They fill the gap in the education of these children who have had to drop out from school after the seventh standard to start working. We have been very happy with our experience with Masoom. The children in one of the schools supported by TMF work in a leather factory during the day and are thrilled at the opportunity to finish their schooling.

9

Educational Initiatives in Bangalore

At the inaugural meeting of the TMF board of directors, Bangalore was not included within the cities to be covered by TMF. The primary credit for persuading the top leadership of the Foundation to change this policy goes to Vasudha Ravichandran. Married to one of Tech Mahindra's most senior executives, the Bangalore-based Ravichandran, Vasudha kept up a continuous stream of appeals on behalf of Bangalore NGOs. Her pleas were finally acceded to. For the first three years, the Bangalore work was handled by her single-handed, on a purely voluntary basis. After a careful search, we recruited Mamatha Esteves, a bright, well-qualified young woman to assist her. She joined us on 1 January 2009.

Parikrma Humanity Foundation

One of our first partners in Bangalore was Parikrma, which went on to become one of our stars. We mentioned in Chapter 3 the important new initiative, Parikrma Education Transformation Centre, which TMF has just joined in an attempt to bring about improvement in municipal schools of Bangalore. Here we shall introduce their school which first gave us an insight into their amazing work.

Led by the indomitable Shukla Bose, Parikrma describes its educational philosophy in the following terms:

Our education philosophy aims to build character, mould talent and impart skill. We achieve this by doing the following:

- *Empower the child through superior knowledge, values and mental and physical skills*
- *Provide real life experience through an experiential learning programme that captures life skills, real life project work etc.*
- *Allow the child to express oneself through various forms of art*
- *Provide wide exposure across all facets of life*

It follows the ICSE (Indian Certificate of Secondary Education) curriculum. The language of instruction is English with Kannada (the local language) as the second language. In the proposal, Parikrma informed us that the ICSE board had conferred on them an award for Excellence in Education and Human Enrichment in 2004.

Shukla Bose and some Parikrma children

> Parikrma has never looked at TMF as just a donor but as partner in our journey of progress. When Mr Khanna and his team visited one of our schools a few years ago, they took great interest in observing our operations and paid intense attention to our long-term plans. They realized that there was great synergy in our respective visions. They supported our English First programme wherein we laid emphasis on lifting the level of English in our schools by first training the teachers. With their financial support we were able to bring in some of the best English trainers from British Council to get our teachers upgrade their knowledge of both spoken and written English. Then last year they partly sponsored the operational costs of one of our schools which we proudly call Parikrma Centre for Learning supported by Tech Mahindra.
>
> The biggest strength of this Foundation is that they have listened to us and tried to match our needs rather than giving us what was convenient for them.
>
> Shukla Bose, Parikrma

To a large extent, the secret of Parikrma's success lies in the close attention it pays to the child's physical and social well-being. The school provides the children a well-balanced diet with the aim of ensuring that the child gets at least 80 per cent of its calorie needs in the school itself. The healthcare programme covers immunization, regular health check-ups and where necessary hospitalization. Psychological counselling is arranged for children who have been through traumatic experiences.

Recognizing the crucial importance of a nurturing environment at home for the overall development of the child, it has actively sought to forge a close link with the community from which the children come.

Its model, called 'Circle of Life', aims to support the child even at the post school stage, be it a professional college or a vocational course.

Parikrma has devoted much attention to achieving the objective of ensuring that children get excellent English-language education. As we have seen, this is a nationwide challenge, given the background of the children where nobody in the family or the community speaks English. All too often, the teachers themselves lack adequate proficiency to teach English to these children. With the help of support from

TMF and external experts trained by the British Council, an ambitious capacity building programme was undertaken. This has made the English-teaching competence of the teachers truly impressive. Parikrma has devised many different ways to get teachers to inculcate in the children a love for the language. Debating, movies, spelling bee, storytelling, creative writing etc. are used across their four centres.

The outstanding success of this programme made the later decision to accept the proposal to sponsor one of their four centres, the Sahakarnagar Centre—a proposal strongly supported by our manager Mamatha—an easy one. We agreed with her assessment that this partnership will enable us to radically transform the lives of children attending the centre. Backed by the continued dedicated and imaginative leadership of Shukla Bose, Parikrma has with sound understanding of pedagogic principles, transparent empathy with children from underprivileged backgrounds and highly trained teachers produced English-language education institution of a standard that can hold its own with any 'five star' school.

Children are exposed to art, drama, theatre, classical music and dance and sports as part of the curriculum, most of which are compulsory. Children who do well in any of these are given intense training so they can excel further. They have participated in national and international events and brought many laurels to Parikrma.

Parent-teacher meetings are held once every three months with almost 100 per cent attendance!

Usually, when one asks children from low income families what their life ambition is, they, like any other their age, mention a career they have learnt to admire in the course of their limited experience. Alas, all too often there seems little correlation between the stated goal and the likely eventual achievement. Parikrma is amongst the schools where it is difficult to see any such significant gap between the children's aspiration and what they can realistically be expected to achieve. Given their academic achievement and personality development, they appear perfectly capable of surmounting the hurdles which the economic and social conditions of their families may confront them with. I recall, for instance, my conversation with two sisters, one in the fourth and the other in the six. Their father earns Rs 5000 as a labourer and mother Rs 2000 by taking tailoring jobs at home. As I talked to them, and heard them spell out their future plans, I saw no reason to doubt the achievability of their respective ambitions to be an IAS officer (failing which, a lawyer) and a doctor.

The Parikrma model proudly refutes the widespread belief that the poor do not value what they get free. The school is absolutely free and yet has practically 100 per cent attendance. The parents, many of whom come from neighbouring slums—though there are also children who come by government bus from as far away as three kilometres—display a striking sense of involvement in their children's education in Parikrma. In fact, one of the mothers, a lowly paid contract worker married to a casual labourer, had an interesting answer to my query about how, in her perception, the education of her child would compare with what her neighbours' children were getting in fee-paying schools. She replied that while she took keen interest in her child's education, her neighbours who sent their children to fee-paying schools did not. The latter's attitude was that they had fulfilled their duty by paying the fees; the rest was the teacher's responsibility! In another case, I witnessed a lively debate between the father and mother of a bright girl. While both were agreed that she should study as far as she was capable of going, they disagreed on what constituted an ideal future for her. The father argued in favour of the security of a government job while the mother felt there would be faster merit-based progress in a private firm. Happily, neither restricted their vision to finding a good husband for her!

Many a parent in the troubled North-east region, fearing for the future of their children—threatened either by militants or security forces or both—have sent them to study in what they have a right to expect would be safe havens. Lalcha is one such youth. Thanks to his own ability and hard work and aided and encouraged by Parikrma, he is now a student in the prestigious National Law School in Bangalore.

Parikrma would very much like to use their experience and skills to help improve quality of government schools. Shukla does not subscribe to the conventional wisdom that the problem lies only with the teachers. In fact, she has demonstrated on a small scale that the quality of learning can improve in a government school using the very same teachers. The problem, she tells me, also lies in management. 'It is a leadership issue.' As with so much else in the country, the problems of government schools can also be traced back to political leadership and bureaucracy which all too often lack understanding of the issues involved and the will to change.

Jeevodaya, Bangalore

All our partners serve those who are in some way disadvantaged, be it economically, socially or physically, and often in more ways than one. But perhaps few have reached out to the poorest of the poor with the determination of Father Gerard of Bangalore. For more than twenty years, his charitable organization Jeevodaya has run education programmes for deprived children of the slums of Bangalore. The most outstanding of Jeevodaya's undertakings, and the one with which TMF is associated, is the relatively recently established Divine Mercy Learning Centre.

Many students of this school are children of bonded labour, sweating away in a nearby quarry. A few are abandoned children or orphans, others are children of widowed or deserted mothers. As parents can't find a functioning school around the area, their children either accompany them to quarries while the slightly older female children start working as house maids. This has led to a cycle of poverty. Into this profoundly challenging setting, arrived Father Gerard, offering free and good-quality education to the children. With the help of donors, one of whom gifted him a two acre plot of land, Jeevodaya has built the Divine Mercy Learning Centre from scratch. It is an English-medium school for 250 of these truly marginalized children.

The school is situated on the outskirts of Bangalore. Transportation was a big issue. With TMF funding, the school was able to buy a fifty-seater bus at a subsidized rate. With the assistance of TMF, it was also able to create a library, a computer lab and start regular PT classes.

Fr Gerard and a rising star

The Divine Mercy Learning Centre seeks to make children proficient in three languages: English, Kannada and Hindi. For this purpose, it has specialized teachers who have been well trained to handle language classes. They make extensive use of the audio-visual room, also set up with TMF assistance, to teach children. Father Gerard proudly displays to visitors the little children's competence in English and mathematics.

A visit to the quarry revealed that practically every mother was illiterate but every one of them was determined that their children, be they boys or girls, would be educated and empowered to lead a life totally different from the one inflicted on them.

To quote from one of the reports from our Bangalore executive, 'During my visits to the school, I have observed that the teachers are enthusiastic, disciplined and care for the children. The children enjoy being at school, given their conditions back home.' When Father Gerard was asked about the criteria he employed while recruiting his highly motivated and

'We love coming to school'

A parent, and the quarry he works in

dedicated teachers, he replied, 'Of course, they must be qualified but, equally importantly, they must be keen to teach the poor.'

Given the often traumatic experiences which children coming to this school suffer at home, TMF has also acceded to Father Gerard's request for funding a counsellor.

Like any good school, Divine Mercy Learning Centre has an efficient and well-conceptualized monitoring and evaluation mechanism. It also has excellent relations with the community and remains in regular touch with the parents. Asked about sustainability, Father Gerard says they have plans to have a notebook manufacturing unit and a dairy farm. They are already cultivating vegetables, pulses and ragi.

Of course, this school still has some way to go before it can be put in the same rank as, say, Parikrma but it appears to be showing consistent improvement.

Raza Educational And Social Welfare Society

Benazeer Baig, the gentle revolutionary of Bismillah Nagar, Bangalore, is the founder of Raza Educational and Social Welfare society. Her inspiring journey began in 1994. Bismillah Nagar was a scrap centre where all sorts of metallic scrap was broken down and traded. The colony, largely Muslim, was also home

Benazeer

to many small factories and garages with inhuman working conditions. What moved her was the sight of young boys working in these factories. Not only were these children deprived of an opportunity to study, the hazardous work environment inflicted terrible damage to their health. Benazeer took upon herself the challenge of eradicating this callous exploitation of children. Thus was born Raza.

Like all those struggling to wipe out the disgraceful practice of child labour, Benazeer had to confront the threats of factory owners. And then there was the struggle to convince parents to allow the child to study rather than see them as a source of additional income for the family.

Research has convincingly established the relationship between education and the eradication of child labour. Hearing a thought-provoking lecture by Prof. Myron Wiener of MIT in 1990 altered my own thinking on child labour. He argued persuasively that the most effective antidote to child labour, and indeed the community's economic advancement, is universalization of education without waiting for family incomes to go up. He cited ample empirical evidence from other parts of the world in favour of this proposition. He felt that this had special reference to a country like India where child labour was rampant. Later, Weiner spelt out his argument comprehensively in his classic work *The Child and the State in India: Child Labor and Education Policy in Comparative Perspective*.

With the help of a Rotary Club, Benazeer established a school offering children low cost, and where necessitated by the child's family circumstances, free education. To this was added vocational training to their mothers and siblings to enable them to earn a respectable living.

At any given time the Excellent school, which is how she named her school, educates close to 600 students with

Experience with TMF

Tech Mahindra Foundation is an incredible foundation. In my life it was turning point to work with TMF because they made me a professional in all the levels in all fields. Mamatha ma'am, I am really thankful to you for making me professional Social Worker. TMF has made us learn, improve and march towards success of organization.

Khanna Sir is inspiring and encouraging personality. He encouraged us to achieve our goal with his energy which makes you work hard and achieve your goal. He is a person with vast experience and understanding of social issues.

I feel I am very lucky because I got to know all these people through TMF.

It is very rare in any foundation where you get total freedom to work for your own project & make your own budget, what you need and how much you need. I feel that is amazing.

TMF is only one foundation which does not just fund you but helps you to grow, learn & become EXCELLENT. There is always direct contact with TMF officer, you can talk to them, share with them, discuss any problem. They are always there to help you.

Benazeer

varying backgrounds. More than 60 per cent students of the school are girls. The medium of instruction is English from LKG to the tenth standard.

Raza continues to run educational programmes under the National Child Labour Project scheme for children identified as child labourers and school dropouts. They are at most times mainstreamed in Excellent school itself in age appropriate classes, or else trained in other vocations.

TMF has collaborated enthusiastically with Benazeer to improve the quality of education in the school. On Mamatha's recommendation, we have supported the schools' science lab, improved teaching of English and sports besides given a substantial grant to cover the cost of books, stationery and other learning materials for the students.

A significant feature of Benazeer's approach to her work is forging partnerships with other NGOs who can assist the school in specific area of need.

Benazeer faces a complex social situation, some elements of which assist her and some oppose. She skilfully leverages the former and bravely confronts the latter. The latter includes the hostile attitude of conservative elements who oppose the idea of a woman taking the lead in a project of this nature. Under her leadership, Raza has become a dynamic force for change in this otherwise rather orthodox Muslim community. It has succeeded in taking the message of education to parents of girls. Child labour has come down significantly. Benazeer is realistic enough to realize that the family income needs to be compensated for the loss of earnings when a child stops working. We shall see in the chapter on vocational training how she has sought to deal with this issue.

Walking through Bismillah Nagar, accompanied by an Excellent teacher and a group of students, I witnessed first-hand the social changes taking place. The first house we entered belonged to a coolie and his housewife spouse, parents of a ninth standard Excellent school student. The mother declared in no uncertain terms that her daughter will study till whatever level she likes and not be hurried into marriage as she herself, a seventh standard dropout, had been. In the next house, the widowed mother of a tenth standard fifteen-year-old confidently backed her brilliant daughter's aspiration to be a lawyer. In the neighbouring tenement, defying stereotypes, a fourteen-year-old declared, as her mother looked on with approving pride, her ambition to be an airhostess.

Located as they are in Bangalore, not surprisingly many aspire to become software engineers. Among them is Azam whose father is unfortunately not able to work and the sole breadwinner is his mother, a vendor.

I spent one very pleasurable morning witnessing a football game between the Muslim girl students, suitably attired to meet the norms of all but the most conservative, but with enough freedom to play with aplomb. Their skills may still have scope

'Raza and my determined mother will give me a great future'

for improvement but their enthusiasm was no less than those of my grand-daughters playing soccer for their schools in the US.

Raza students displaying their soccer skills

Swami Vivekananda Youth Movement (SVYM): Viveka Scholar Programme

SVYM, a not-for profit development organization, in collaboration with the highly reputed Deeksha College, is running the Viveka Scholar Programme, an imaginative scholarship project for bright economically challenged children. It gives them an opportunity, through high quality teaching, to excel in pre-university class (PUC) in science. TMF is supporting 60 girls studying in the first and second years of PUC.

To educate a child in science costs SVYM Rs 32,500 per year. A little more than 45 per cent of the cost is borne by the parents and SVYM. TMF covers 55 per cent of the costs. Deeksha College lends it brand name and human resources, while SVYM manages and monitors the progress of children. All the children are from government schools and belong to the poorer section. The college is well equipped with labs, computers and libraries. Sports and extracurricular activities are compulsory along with other activities. The faculty is well qualified and dedicated.

This is a relatively new addition to our portfolio starting with academic year 2012–13.

10

Vocational Training

There has been growing concern that what was not too long ago confidently predicted as India's demographic dividend—given the projected age structure of the population—may turn out to be a demographic nightmare. While in other major economies, including China, aging populations are entering the period of declining working-age ratios, India is on the eve of a prolonged period of favourable demographics. But it is obvious that this transition will not automatically propel India to significant economic growth and equity. Some other factors are essential, of which one of the most important is that the young should have appropriate skills demanded by a modern economy.

TMF has been deeply aware that critical to a person's empowerment is possession of skills which enables her/him to earn a decent livelihood. Vocational training had been one of TMF's major intervention areas almost since inception, with several excellent partners and programmes to its credit. However, at the end of five years, a need was felt to streamline these efforts through a consistent, unified programme that the Foundation could call its own, and institutionalize a few best practices in the process. This was made possible through the Skills-for-Market Training programme, or simply, the SMART programme.

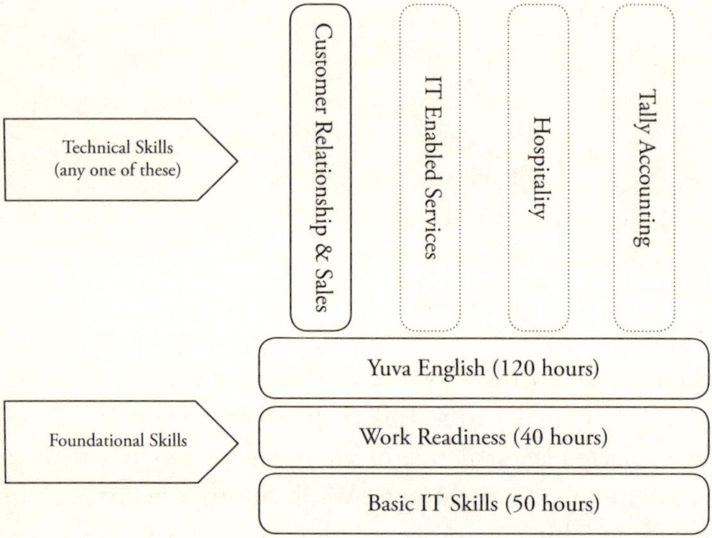

Diagram: The Tech Mahindra SMART Programme

Tech Mahindra SMART focuses on skills that are marketable, and establishes a set of consistent practices that can be replicated across different cities. SMART is being consciously developed as a programme with a strong element of quality at its core. This quality is being driven by a robust set of processes for each component of the programme—from identification of the NGO partner to selection and training of the students and finally to placing them in appropriate jobs and tracking them after they have been placed. TMF has engaged the services of Edulever, a specialized agency that has been working in the vocational training sector for some time, to develop the programme tools necessary to ensure consistent high quality for the programme.

SMART programme is a three-month one, with a batch size not exceeding 25 students.

Yuva English—TMF's existing English learning programme developed in partnership with the Centre for Learning

Resources, Pune—has been embedded into the SMART programme. Students enrolling at a SMART centre are taken through the three foundational courses, and then the appropriate technical course is introduced. Training delivery is based on the 'Learning by Doing' approach, which implies that the curriculum comprises a series of interactive activities, tasks, role plays, projects, and assignments that the students are expected to accomplish as part of the course.

Another very important part of the SMART programme is its inclusive nature; it caters to persons with disabilities as well. For this, TMF is partnering with NGOs that have been working in the PWD (people with disabilities) space, and inducting them into the Tech Mahindra-SMART programme, tentatively called 'SMART *plus*'.

The SMART programme clearly aims at improving the employment prospects of underprivileged youth in the new economy jobs. Hence, the success of the programme will be measured by the number of youth who are successfully trained and gainfully employed in various sectors such as retail, IT enabled services, hospitality etc. To ensure this, proactive efforts for creating linkages with potential employers are already in place, and it is expected that a national network of employers will be developed who will be active recruiters from Tech Mahindra-SMART centres. The programme aims at a minimum of 70 per cent students getting placed at the end. Students, once placed, will be tracked for a period of at least six months to ensure that they have settled comfortably in their jobs and are taking the right steps for their career progression. In addition to employment, self-employment will also be added as a specific outcome in the course of developing the programme.

The programme started with three centres (two in Hyderabad and one in the national capital region, NCR) in October 2012, and expanded to 14 by April 2013 and to 24 by December 2013. The number of centres is expected to double in 2014–15, and eventually reach 100 by 2016–17.

Some of the centres are run by old partners; many new organizations have come within the SMART ambit. The search is on for many more. Indeed, Tech Mahindra SMART has already become one of the flagship programmes of the Foundation.

List of SMART Partners (as on 31 Dec 2013)

S. No.	*Name of partner*	*Location*	*No. of centres*	*Whether new or old TMF partner*
1.	Yugantar	Hyderabad	2	New
2.	Agrasar	Delhi NCR	2	New
3.	Ank	Delhi NCR	1	Old
4.	RISE India	Delhi NCR	1	New
5.	SEWA	Delhi NCR	1	Old
6.	Saarthak	Delhi NCR	1	Old
7.	APSA	Hyderabad	2	New
8.	Cadre	Hyderabad	2	New
9.	Deaf Enabled Foundation	Hyderabad	1	New
10.	Aarohan	Bhubaneswar	1	New
11.	Enable India Foundation	Bangalore	1	Old
12.	SNEHA	Mumbai	1	Old
13.	Reach India	Kolkata	1	New
14.	SEOMP	Kolkata	1	New
15.	YWCA	Chennai	1	New
16.	Don Bosco	Chennai	1	New
17.	Aide-et-Action	Chennai	1	New
18.	BREADS	Bangalore	1	New
19.	Shishu Mandir	Bangalore	1	New
20.	Nirman	Pune	1	New
	Total		24	

Some Tech Mahindra SMART Success stories

Let us cite just three of the hundreds of lives which have been transformed by Tech Mahindra SMART centres:

Siddarth, a young lad barely out of his teens, coming from a family facing financial difficulties, is now an important member of a real estate company after attending a Tech Mahindra SMART centre in Gurgaon. Displaying maturity well beyond his years, he says, 'I can now think differently, weigh alternatives in different perspectives and act thoughtfully.'

Belonging to a seven-member family dependent on the meagre earnings of a father who is a daily wage labourer, Bandi Devika Rani and her sister have brought financial security to their family by getting reasonably well-paying jobs after attending a SMART centre in Hyderabad.

Manisha, who had never worked on a computer before, can now proudly declare that she works for a well-known hospital in Delhi thanks to the skills acquired in a SMART centre located in Hasanpur, Delhi.

Pre-Tech Mahindra SMART period

Let us briefly survey the work done in the field of vocational training in the five years preceding the introduction of the Tech Mahindra SMART programme.

Unnati

One of TMF's most consistently successful vocational training partner was Unnati in Bangalore. Run by SGBS Trust, it has the advantage of excellent infrastructure gifted to it by some generous donors. While most of our other partners have to work out of rented space of limited size, Unnati has a well-designed building of its own, with adequate space. What has further contributed to its success is the fact that some of its trustees are businessmen with first hand knowledge of market requirements. And finally, Ramesh Swamy, the 'lead trustee' takes keen personal interest.

Unnati trains economically disadvantaged youth aged eighteen and above in vocational and life skills, making them employable in seventy days' time with an assured job at the end of training. It has successfully trained and placed batch after batch in reputed companies with good salaries and social securities. From 2008–11, they trained 1000 youth; of these, TMF sponsored the training of more than 250 young boys and girls.

There is constant debate within the Foundation on whether vocational training facilities should be provided free of charge or for a fee. Some would argue that eventually a NGO must recover the entire cost from the beneficiary to ensure its sustainability. Others feel that the fee should be nominal, requiring some continuing financial support to the NGO by a funding agency. Others prefer some sort of a low or no interest loan programme, repayment to be made in easy instalments once the trainee has got a regular job.

Many of those who recommend that some fees must be charged believe that any free facility is not appreciated and the trainee will not be serious. Unnati's experience contradicts this assumption. The entire training and facilities are provided free of cost to the youth. Bus passes, food and stay (for outstation youth) are extended. On several visits to Unnati, I invariably found the students alert and conscientious, under the watchful eye of their trainers who were performing their duties with a great sense of commitment. Ramesh explained that they have paid a lot of attention to discipline and the willingness to work long hours if need be.

It is not at all surprising to learn while talking to a couple of ex-students that the training received at Unnati had taken them from failure to get a job to very satisfactory employment, at reasonable salaries.

So well established is Unnati in the field that companies come there for 'campus recruitment'.

Unnati has vision of a million youth trained through its model and has now started a vigorous replication drive in different parts of the country.

A typical Unnati success story

Lata, twenty-six, had discontinued her studies just after she had finished her seventh standard. Hailing from a poor family in rural Bangalore, her mother got her married early. Her husband soon deserted her and Lata was left with a baby girl and was back at her parents house. Her mother, who works for an NGO as a helper, told her about Unnati. Hoping that things would be better, Lata joined the retail training course.

The faculty at Unnati remembers Lata as a good student who was always eager to learn. She was initially hesitant to speak in English. However, she was encouraged to soon start trying. In just seventy days, she was confident and ready for placements. Lata got placed at Kati Zone, a retail food outlet, during campus placements. This seventh standard dropout is now a cashier at the outlet and earns a good salary. Lata says confidently, 'I am now scared of no one and have enough confidence to give my daughter a good future.'

Nirmala Niketan

Nirmala Niketan is a regular college in Mumbai awarding diplomas and degrees. It has acquired the reputation of producing quality professional social workers with sound understanding of social problems and a deep commitment to the underprivileged with, to quote from its literature, 'a vision closely focused on empowerment of the vulnerable and exploited groups in society'. And so TMF was immediately interested in a proposal from Nirmala Niketan to fund scholarships for some students who could not afford even the modest fees of the college but had a sincere desire to take up social work as a career.

Talking a couple of years later to some recipients of TMF scholarships convinced us that they will indeed devote their lives to help those whose lives had been rendered miserable by cruel circumstances beyond their control. Take for instance the life story of a twenty-one-year Muslim girl, whose father, a construction labourer, abandoned the family about ten years ago and who had to join her seven siblings in assisting their mother in cleaning fish to survive. But, by sheer guts, she has made her way through college and now is training to become a counsellor for institutionalized girls. As she herself has had to live in a rescue home, she has a deep understanding of the potentially life-destroying problems these girls have to encounter.

There is another girl, the daughter of a cobbler, who was helped by the TMF scholarship to acquire a diploma in social work, a stepping stone to fulfil her dream to help the poor whose multiple problems she has seen at close quarters.

Another TMF scholar, a boy who had witnessed terrible scenes of wife beating in the slum he lived in, with neither the police nor neighbours willing to intervene, has decided to take up the challenge of dealing with domestic violence as his career option.

It is a measure of the quality and perspectives of our scholars that some of them have been selected for Gandhi Fellowships, an intensive two-year programme funded by the Ajay Piramal Foundation designed to produce young men and women who will be able and willing to take up leadership roles in various fields.

Raza

We have in an earlier chapter referred to our partnership with the NGO Raza in Bangalore. The intrepid Benazeer has not limited her work for the Muslim slum community, whose welfare has become her life mission, to the school we mentioned earlier.

Talking to parents, especially mothers, she realized that unless the family income is substantially increased, child labour will continue to persist. So she has also established a vocational training centre.

The young men and women who train under Raza's vocational training courses come from varied backgrounds. A few would already be working at some place, earning a small, unsatisfactory salary; others would be living alarmingly below the poverty line and struggling to make ends meet. Then there are girls whose conservative communities do not permit them any aspirations outside the four confines of the house.

In the last three years, Raza's 'Excellent Vocational Centre' has trained more than 800 youth who are now working with companies like Big Bazaar, Forum, Westside, McDonald's, Café Coffee Day and SPAR. This is apart from the tailoring skills given to 200 older women every year.

With the help of Unnati, the commitment to workplace ethics and etiquette has become a valuable part of the training. Benazeer informed us with pride that so strict has been the instilling of discipline that classes went on as usual even during Ramzan.

We shall have more to say about volunteering by TMF associates in a later chapter. Here we would like to place on record the valuable help rendered by one of Tech Mahindra's retired vice presidents, A.K. Prasad. According to TMF's Bangalore manager, he was a regular volunteer helping Raza set up management and accounting procedures. This has helped Raza develop from an informal centre to a professional institution.

While Benazeer is generous in acknowledging the support of TMF and help from others, the credit of overcoming multiple problems goes primarily to her and her team. It is they who convinced conservative husbands and fathers to change their mindset on the potential economic and social role of women. Again, it was often not easy to persuade young women conditioned by their patriarchical environments to step out and become confident skilled entrants into the market place. Many emerged without abandoning the burqa, but like Benazeer herself, not really conforming to stereotypes associated with burqas.

But Benazeer is not one to rest on her laurels. On my last visit to her she spelt out her plans to set up Raza/Excellent's own commercial enterprises where some of the trainees would be absorbed and indeed become entrepreneurs.

This vocational centre will soon join the Tech Mahindra SMART family.

Namdevrao Suryawashi Technical School

A passing reference is in order about one particular initiative. The reader may recall that one partner we referred to in our chapter dealing with educational programmes run by our NGO partners in Pune was the K.B. Hire School

Most children of this school come from a low economic class and are under tremendous pressure to start supporting their families after completing tenth standard. Due to lack of financial support, formal training and proper guidance, they tend to join low paid jobs available in the market condemning them to remain in poverty-like situation. To break this vicious cycle, the school along with TMF decided to support a certain number of them so they could undergo industrial training in the Namdevrao Suryawashi Technical School located in the same campus and run by the same organization as the school. It offers a choice of trades such as welder, fitter, electrician and motor mechanic. A discussion with the faculty was reassuring. They spoke highly of the commitment of these trainees and their prospects.

Ank

Led by a young husband–wife team, Abhishek and Jyoti, Ank was earlier TMF's partner for teaching English to youth using Yuva English of which we spoke earlier. It has now qualified to become a Tech Mahindra SMART centre.

Ank students practicing spoken English via Yuva English role play technique

Abhishek, the head of the institute masters the Tech Mahindra SMART manuals

Occasional Hiccup

We did support a few other initiatives but they were not always very successful. It was also in this field that we had a rare case of an NGO partner proving to be less than honest; this led to premature termination of partnership. They gave us false information about their placement record.

The Legacy of Mahindra Satyam Foundation

Our work in this field was significantly enlarged when the Mahindra Satyam Foundation (MSF) came on board because livelihoods had been a major focus area of the old Satyam Foundation. We decided that we would continue this tradition even during the period in which MSF was going through financial stringency.

As a part of its livelihoods programme, MSF operated vocational training schools in a number of cities to provide free training to school dropouts, unemployed youth from economically backward sections, including persons with disabilities. They impart basic IT skill training along with communicative English and English typing to unemployed youth and assist them in finding jobs.

These were called IT schools. I visited the IT school run by MSF—now merged with TMF—in Koti, Hyderabad, more than once and was always impressed by the commitment and skills of the teachers and the seriousness with which the students attended the classes. One day in July 2012, I decided to sit down for a detailed chat with some of the past 'graduates' of this IT school to see where they were today. It was immensely gratifying to see that in many cases the skills acquired in the school had transformed their lives, either enabling them to get their first job or substantially raising their earning capacity. There was this bright Muslim girl, barely eighteen, who attributes her success in getting a job as a telecaller to the skills and confidence acquired at the IT school. A twenty-five-year-old young woman was earning sufficient salary to withstand the harassment of her in-laws. A nineteen-year-old boy, son of a casual labourer, and himself an intermediate pass, had just finished the course and recounted his joy in capturing a well-paid job. Then there was the heart-warming experience of an orphan nineteen-year-old girl, who had been recruited by the Mahindra Satyam BPO after finishing her stint at the IT school some eight months ago. One young person after another expressed her/his gratitude to MSF for empowering them to enter the job market with confidence.

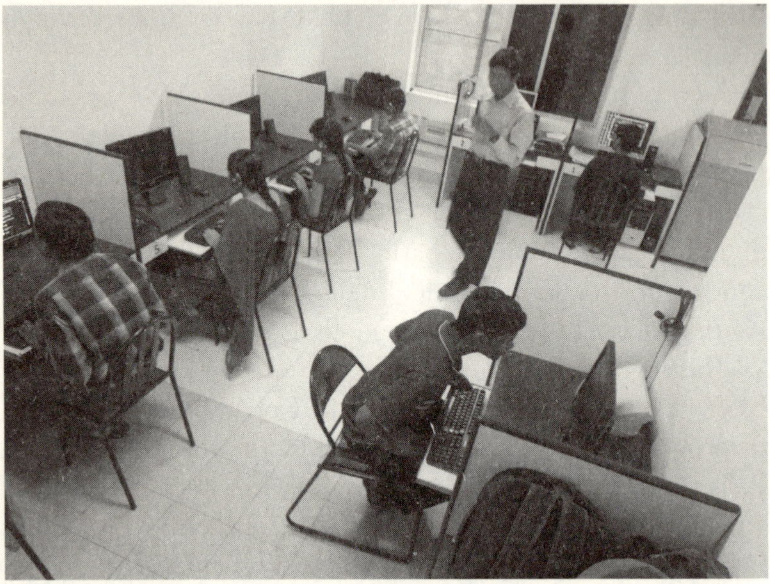

'Tech Mahindra SMART skills will ensure our employability'

In Pune, there are two IT schools whose management was taken over by TMF when it was decided to shut down MSF's unit in this city as an economy measure.

These IT institutes have joined the Tech Mahindra SMART fraternity.

Our engagement with vocational training programmes run specifically either for women or physically challenged will be covered in subsequent chapters.

11

Women's Empowerment

There is something profoundly embarrassing about the 2013 Global Gender Gap Index released by the World Economic Forum. India ranked a lowly 101st of 136 countries covered by the index, indicating a huge disparity in the access of women to economic, political, educational and health opportunities.

All programmes supported by TMF are gender sensitive. Going beyond that general principle, some partners have been chosen specifically because they run impressive women empowerment programmes. In the case of women, true empowerment requires a range of inputs, including control over economic resources, awareness of rights and gender sensitization. But of all the inputs, perhaps the most important and fundamental is education, though naturally it is not sufficient by itself. And, as we have mentioned before, in the term 'education' we also include vocational skills which would enable a woman to be economically independent.

We have been fortunate to locate some very good organizations sharing our vision of women's empowerment.

Katalyst

Our constant concern has been to reach out to the maximum number of beneficiaries by keeping per capita cost as low as possible. But here was a scholarship programme for very bright girls from low income backgrounds that would involve an average of Rs 50,000 per year per head. So, initially, we were a bit hesitant. The persistence of our Bangalore team persuaded us to take a closer look. An analysis of the break-up of Rs 50,000 made the budget look more reasonable than at first sight. It covered college fees in well-known institutes of higher education, in many cases hostel fees, medical insurance, books, computer, and, where necessary, good coaching classes.

What has further enhanced the quality of this programme is that these girls get counselling from experts and mentoring by professionals from some of the most famous companies in Bangalore.

Our Bangalore executives have also satisfied themselves that truly deserving candidates were selected after a careful evaluation of their academic achievements and economic circumstances, which included not only a study of the relevant documents but also visits to their homes and colleges.

When the first examination results came in a year after we launched our partnership with Katalyst, we were greatly encouraged. All of them had done very well and some brilliantly.

I have more than once met the girls collectively and have been impressed by their high ability combined with determination to do well in future. On my last visit to Bangalore, I decided to visit some of them in their houses for in-depth interviews with them and, equally importantly, their families.

The first girl I was taken to meet was Shabnam, a final year student in electronics and communication stream of BE. She comes from a conventional Muslim family and lives in a slum dominated by Muslim population where most children drop out of school before the tenth. With a brilliant academic record, she became the first girl in her neighbourhood to enter an engineering college. Happily, her father supports her higher education. He is a driver and mother a housewife.

It is a measure of Shabnam's level-headedness that she opted for the lower starting salary from the job offers she received through campus interviews from two well-known companies because the one she chose has a better reputation and does the sort of things she sees herself as happy doing.

I was told that Shabnam has excelled in computer skills like C, C++, Java, Data Structure. What I could see for myself were her soft skills, which would clearly make her at home in any setting, no matter how different it may be from the modest environment in which she grew up.

Shabnam:an inspiration to other girls in the community

Shabnam would like to be ambassador in her community for children to continue their studies. We confidently hope that she will be an inspiration to other girls of the community and her family's vision will be shared by a larger number of parents who will be encouraged to support the aspirations of their bright daughters.

Equally impressive is Anushree A. Ganjam. It is difficult to believe that there was a time when she, to quote her, 'had too much of stage fear and didn't have much hold on English language' and

Anushree and her proud mother

that she 'wasn't good in communication too'. Today, she speaks with remarkable self-confidence and fluency. She comes from a family whose economic status had come crashing down for reasons which need not detain us here. This twenty-three-year-old, now working for a leading multinational telecom company, has, despite her relative youth, already helped transform the economic and social condition of her family.

Now a fully qualified computer engineer, Anushree, who seemed to have never scored below 90 per cent in any of her examinations, acknowledges with touching humility how the visits of TMF executives encouraged her and how the TMF-funded Katalyst programme has put her on the road to achieving her aspirations. Her ultimate aim is to be an astrophysicist in NASA. Given her academic achievements, all the skills she has acquired with the help of Katalyst, and above all her own innate qualities, it does not appear to be an unrealistic dream at all.

Shabnam and Anushree are only two of the more than hundred girls who have been recipients of this scholarship from TMF.

Excerpts from a note by Anushree A. Ganjam

I joined Katalyst in 2009 when I was in 4th semester of BE. It's been really a great and memorable experience since then.

Earlier I had too much of stage fear and didn't have much hold on English language. I wasn't good in communication too.

After I joined Katalyst, I found everybody in Katalyst are just like me. Everybody had financial problems in family and everybody has that urge to achieve something different . . .

Katalyst made me understand that life is not only about studies and marks, but also identifying our own inner talents and how to use this talent to achieve more.

I'm happy to say that Katalyst provided me a mentor who has a vast knowledge in my area of interest. He provided me books to read and also various links (websites) to refer to know about what are the developments happening in Outer space.

The access to internet supported by Katalyst also helped me gain more knowledge on current affairs and technologies as we know that the world is changing very fast.

Also industrial visit to Tech Mahindra (AMR Techpark, Bangalore) and TCS (ITPL, Bangalore) helped me to learn more on corporate life.

I have met Mamatha Esteves from Tech Mahindra Foundation when she had come for house visit in 2009. She was very humble to my parents. Since my mother didn't know English, she spoke in Kannada to her and listened to all our problems. I really respect her effort to meet me personally and help me out in everything.

I have also met other people from Tech Mahindra Foundation in Katalyst office 3–4 times. I found them very humble, encouraging and I really respect their effort and love towards the society which they do as a part of corporate social responsibility. After seeing this great work being done by TMF and Katalyst, all of us feel even we need to give back something to this society. I will definitely do this in a few years down the line.

Today I'm proud to be a girl and I can confidently face anything that comes in life. The credit goes to Katalyst for all the strength that I have at present and for what I'm today. Katalyst not only helped me financially but it has also helped me become mentally strong.

My aim is to excel in the field of Astrophysics.

I would also like to say, when I look back at my life now, it is Katalyst and Tech Mahindra Foundation that will be remembered because they both have played an important role in my career.

Regards
Anushree A. Ganjam

SPRJK (Shri Pandit Ratnachandraji Jain Kanyashala Trust)

When our then manager in Mumbai, Sejal Mody, described to us the work that SPRJ Kanyashala was doing, it immediately appealed to us as a potential partner. Over the years, it has amply justified our faith. Located in Ghatkopar, this charitable institution founded by a group of Jain philanthropists runs a comprehensive educational institution for underprivileged girls, many of whom belong to the minority community. With the motto *Susanskrit Nari Jagat Kalyankari* (a cultured woman nurtures the world), it operates a school, a college and a wide ranging programme for imparting vocational skills. These courses lead to good careers in fields like fashion designing, beauty, culture and interior designing.

In consultation with the exceedingly well-informed and highly experienced chief executive and trustee Meena Khetani, we conceptualized a project to provide loan scholarships to a number of girls from economically challenged backgrounds doing high quality vocational courses. To quote from the proposal submitted by SPRJK:

Through this project we aim to provide top-quality, affordable, vocational education to underprivileged girls living in the slums and chawls of Mumbai. Education in job-oriented courses will transform their lives, help them realize their full potential and enable them to be economically independent. They can earn a respectable life and bring their families out of the circle of poverty. These girls will ensure that their children get education too. Also, many of them support other poor children to give back to the society what they received. This way, there will be a continuous cycle which will spread education and development. Empowerment of these girls will be an asset to the society and the nation as a whole.

The project involved a loan covering 75 per cent of the fees for the course. The repaid amount does not come back to TMF but is retained by the SPRJK Trust, which creates a revolving fund for supporting more girls in subsequent years. We were delighted when the Trust informed us after the scheme had run for three years that this micro finance project had become self-sustaining with around 85 per cent students already repaying their loans either in installments or after they get jobs.

Diverse backgrounds but same aspiration: acquire skills for an empowered future

Our Mumbai executive Swati has often spoken of the passion of the teachers and the quality of training. The determination and level-headedness of the students whom we have supported in truly impressive.

There is this twenty-two-year-old girl from straitened family circumstances who is a cancer survivor and is now training to be a beautician at SPRJK with the help of a TMF loan. She volunteers at the Tata Memorial Cancer Hospital instilling in cancer patients the belief that they can lead normal lives while recalling how she herself was able to pull herself out from depths of despair.

Another aspiring beautician, a young Muslim girl, speaks with gratitude of her father, a driver, who defied societal pressures to get his daughter married early and has encouraged her to do what she likes.

On each of our visits, the girls who had taken the fashion design course would display with glowing pride what they had learnt

Transformation in Farheen's life:
A) Farheen: outside her home in a slum

under the guidance of their teachers. Their work is exhibited at an annual fashion show to appreciative audiences which include potential future employers. The contrast between the very modest homes they come from and the sophistication of their beautiful creations is stunning. This comes through vividly if you visit Farheen at her home and see her in action on stage.

While our ideal is to instil in these young women the confidence to operate with their newly acquired capabilities in the expanding market place, we have to accept realistically that in some cases their deeply ingrained 'sanskaras' or the social circumstances will not allow them to do so. So, as a second best option, we have to ensure that our partners give them skills which will enable them to earn a dignified living operating out of their homes or in the neighbourhood. Thanks to enhanced tailoring expertise or a beautician's training, many of these girls are able to do just that.

Many more now have the skill and self-belief to open their own boutiques or to go and work with leading interior design houses or fashion designers; these include young women whose families till yesterday would not let their wards out of their sight lest their marriage prospects be ruined!

B) Farheen marches confidently down the ramp with one of her creations

SPRJK is clearly motivated by deep philanthropic concerns derived from their Jain faith, but it is a secular institution, reaching out to the underprivileged of all communities.

SNEHA

Another women's empowerment programme TMF supports in Mumbai is run by Society for Nutrition, Education and Health Action with the very apt acronym SNEHA. It was founded by Dr A. Fernandez, former dean of Sion Hospital. We were introduced to her by Lucius Lobo, a senior TM executive, who has taken keen interest in the work of TMF from its very inception. SNEHA runs several activities designed to impart to slum-dwelling women the skills and confidence to change their lives and to change the lives of people around them. TMF has helped SNEHA undertake training of young women annually as *swasthya sevika*s. This is a certificate course for nursing aides. As Fernandes explained to us in our first meeting with her, there is tremendous demand in private nursing homes for such qualified nursing aides. Having received intensive training, they are placed as interns in hospitals or nursing homes many of which later take them on as permanent employees. Besides giving them financial independence and dramatically altering their status in the family, it gives them a sense of pride at being part of a noble profession.

Take the case of the twenty-five-year-old Shabana. After her tenth from an Urdu-medium school, she spent the next eight years at home as her father, a tailor, would not allow her to go out to work. Her father is now no more. With the backing of her mother, also a tailor, she came to SNEHA. Having gradually overcome inhibitions instilled in her since childhood, she now greatly enjoys her work and is today looking forward to a dignified career.

Another girl, now engaged to be married, revealed shyly that her boyfriend has agreed that she can continue to work after they

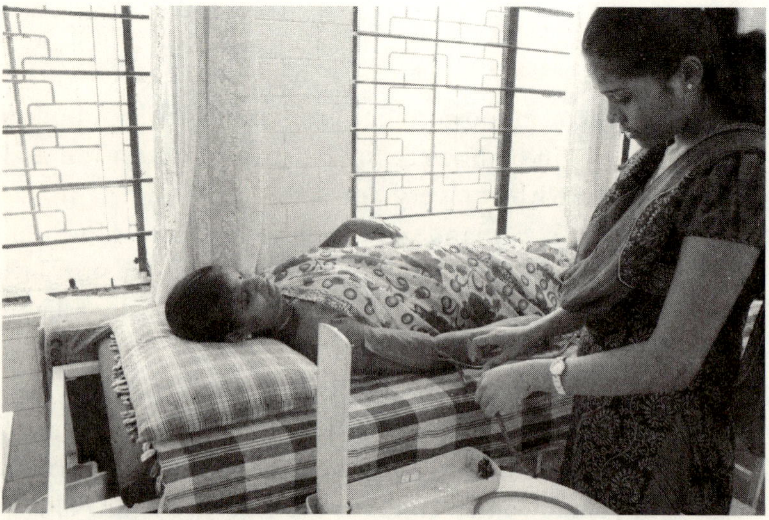

Minakshi with her sphygmomanometer and stethoscope

get married. She said, quite unselfconsciously, that she derives inspiration from the recovery of patients.

It is immensely gratifying to meet girls like Minakshi, daughter of a vendor, who is all set to transform her life and that of her family.

In some cases, the parents had to defy taunts from neighbours and relatives who insinuated that this was not a 'respectable' thing for a girl from a 'good' family to do. One young woman, when asked how her parents reacted to her taking up an unconventional job as a nursing aide, quoted them as saying, 'If because of her, a ninth standard dropout, a life is saved that would be an inspiration for all girls.'

Watching a SNEHA class in action was an enjoyable and educative experience. The girls were absolutely riveted, totally engrossed, eagerly absorbing the lesson. They were clearly headed towards becoming completely reliable nursing aides.

Not surprising, our Mumbai executive reports 100 per cent placement of SNEHA trainees.

SNEHA trainees attentive in class

A word of appreciation from Dr A. Fernandez

SNEHA

Give a woman wings, and she can conquer the world.

The Tech Mahindra Swasthya Sewika Journey at SNEHA harks back to 2009. This was when the first solid steps were taken to set up a program on Nurse Aide training. SNEHA was started by doctors and our work was in public health so this was a very good choice for a vocation for empowering our young women.

Tech Mahindra Foundation supported and encouraged our efforts right from the beginning very wholeheartedly, vesting faith in SNEHA and supporting our dream for young women. The first batch in 2009–2010 had just thirty-six women.

We have since grown in strength with the unflinching support of TMF. The program has to date completed 8 batches covering 219 young women the majority of who are employed. To further enhance the capacities of the women and to make them more employable TMF has also added an English Literacy and Computer skills training component. Since August of 2013, Tech Mahindra now also supports the same initiative in Govandi–Mankhurd areas of Mumbai and there are plans to add more centres in the coming year. We hear the stories of our brave girls and the pride and self-worth and all we can say is . . . *TMF has given our girl's wings.*

Dr Armida Fernandez
Founder Trustee
SNEHA

In August 2013, TMF supported SNEHA in starting a new centre. This centre is located in Govandi which is one of the most vulnerable slum pockets in Mumbai. It is in close proximity to slums like Baiganwadi and Cheetah Camp.

In 2013, SNEHA added two new modules to the nurse aide course. These are Yuva English and basic computers. With the addition of these, both the SNEHA centres are now a part of Tech Mahindra SMART Vocational Training Centres.

Sushrusha

A similar partnership has just begun in Bhubaneswar in partnership with an organization called Sushrusha. Its vision is to give a livelihood to underprivileged young rural women of Bhubaneswar by strengthening their capacity through training them in home nursing. The trainees are generally selected from socially and economically backward classes of the community. Preference is also given to destitute, deprived, divorced and differently abled women who are in urgent need of livelihood support.

TMF was attracted by Sushrusha's track record. In the last nine years, eighteen batches have undergone training as per the training curriculum designed and executed by reputed and experienced doctors, psychiatrists, dieticians, nurses, social workers and behavioural science experts. Thirty previously trained home nurses are also given refresher courses.

This programme meets a growing social need. The elderly, the handicapped and the physically incapacitated are becoming increasingly isolated and helpless. Besides the emotional and financial support they need, these people are physically incapable of taking care of themselves. To give them their dignity, providing home nurses has become essential.

Their proposal to use TMF grant to cover 150 trainees had strong backing by our Bhubaneswar executive who had this to say:

'I see that there is a lot of dedication from the board of trustees and the management who are all on honorary basis . . . Home visits are done before any nurse is placed. Care is taken that the nurses are in constant touch with Shusrusa to update them on the happenings at the place of work. In short, the organization is paving way for the needy destitute women to live an empowered life while at the same time providing for a dignified life for the sick and the elderly who are bedridden. This is a programme worth supporting.'

Nirnaya Trust

An even more recent partner is Nirnaya Trust also of Bhubaneswar. It submitted a proposal for poverty reduction through skill enhancement leading to livelihood for young women. The targeted community is young migrant women in the slums. The reality of their lives is that the families of the migrant community are highly vulnerable, very poorly paid, if given an opportunity to work at all. Lacking any ID proof, they cannot avail of any government subsidies. Their living conditions are dismal and the health and nutrition condition of the family poor. Concretely, the proposal involves support to the skill training centre for tailoring, computer basics, soft skills and hospital/hotel housekeeping.

SEWA

As far as women's empowerment programmes in Delhi are concerned, we had the good fortune of being approached by the renowned SEWA. As is well-known, the Self Employed Women's Association is a women's trade union that was started in Gujarat in 1972 by the distinguished social worker, Ela Bhatt, with the aim of organizing women in the informal sector. It started working in Delhi in 1999, initially concentrating on forming self-help groups. In subsequent years, it has diversified its work significantly. It has grown steadily and today works in a large number of Delhi slums.

We began our partnership with SEWA by supporting their project entitled 'Opening of frontiers of development of adolescent girls and women'. This encompassed four main activities for underprivileged girls:

i. Vocational training: for girls between the age-group of fourteen to twenty-one with courses in embroidery, tailoring and cutting and mehendi.
ii. Soft skill training: in collaboration with the State Bank Academy (SBA) where girls from vocational training programmes got trained in spoken English, basic computers, accountancy etc.

iii. Education: A non-formal education programme for adolescent girls and young women to enable them to have basic reading and writing skills.
iv. Information centre: This performs an invaluable service. It makes available to the slum women information regarding relevant government services and schemes and helps them access these.

Later, we helped SEWA launch a polytechnic for young women. With a syllabus designed by a premier fashion institute, this offers higher quality courses than the normal vocational training programmes in slums. The girls then have a choice between self-employment and placement. SEWA has moved energetically to ensure market linkages.

Thanks to these two TMF-assisted programmes, SEWA Delhi with our help has enabled hundreds of young women to acquire sustainable livelihoods.

Bal Sahyog

Even many long-term residents of Delhi may be unaware that right in the heart of the city, in Connaught Place, is located the headquarters of an NGO founded by Indira Gandhi in1954. It provides on the campus shelter and developmental support to about 100 underprivileged boys. The stewardship of this NGO is now in the hands of a retired IAS officer, Reva Nayyar, the dynamic former secretary of ministry of women and child development.

Designed primarily to ensure the well-being of children in particularly vulnerable circumstances, Bal Sahyog, has enlarged its agenda to address community development issues in some of the difficult slums of Delhi. In 2011, TMF, after a careful evaluation of the potential of this work, decided to support its vocational training programme for women, besides some NFE classes for children. Accredited to the National Institute of Open Schooling, the training of these women covers beauty culture and tailoring and gives them the opportunity to become financially independent.

12

Initiatives to Empower the Visually Impaired

In some ways the most satisfying part of our work has been with respect to empowerment of the physically challenged. Our special emphasis has been on the visually impaired and this deserves a chapter by itself, and a rather long one at that. Our involvement begins at the level of primary school education and goes all the way to life skills and livelihood.

What has added excitement to our work is that the founder-heads of five of our partner NGOs working for the blind are themselves visually impaired.

Fortunately, technology has come to the aid of the visually challenged in a big way and our partners have done terrific work with its help.

Saksham and Dipendra Manocha

There must be few in India who have made as major a contribution as Dipendra to bringing the benefits of IT to the visually impaired. Now in his late forties, Dipendra, son of an engineer, started losing his eyesight when he was twelve. Adjusting bravely to his new condition, he went on to have a brilliant academic record. It was only when he was working for a postgraduate degree in music that he first felt the full force of the handicap confronting a person who had no option but to rely on readers for all the specialized books one needed to read. These were just not available in Braille or any other format accessible to a visually impaired person, making him dependent on readers who were often not around precisely when he needed them. He still remembers the excitement that surged through him when he first touched a computer at the National Association of the Blind (NAB) in R.K. Puram, New Delhi, sometime in December 1993. An understanding flashed through his mind of what IT could do for the blind. He decided there and then that this was the answer he was looking for and made up his mind to devote his life to this mission. It was not an easy decision. Economic consequences were uncertain. Given his academic record, enriched by more than a decade of music training under well-known gurus, it would have been easy for him to get a lecturer's job, thus ensuring economic stability. NAB was hardly in a position to

Dipendra Manocha

offer him that. But his father backed him and Dipendra has not looked back since. In just five years, he and his colleagues were able to set up a high quality computer training centre for the blind in the NAB campus.

In 1999, Dipendra was introduced to the world of digital talking books by Hiroshi Kawamura of Japan at a UNESCAP meeting in Bangkok. He immediately realized its revolutionary potential. When Dipendra first showed us DAISY (Digital Accessible Information System) in action, we were struck by how it would make it dramatically more convenient for a visually impaired person to read even a voluminous book because of the ease with which she could negotiate any text, jumping to any page, moving forward or backward to any portion, something that is difficult in other formats.

At that time, the technology was dependent on a relatively expensive digital talking book player. Dipendra joined the DAISY for All project in 2003 and has played the lead role in evolving a solution bringing the cost down significantly and then disseminating it through the country. He is the managing trustee of our partner Saksham Trust which is working as the secretariat for the DAISY Forum of India. It is promoting networking among and training of organizations producing or distributing content for the visually challenged in Braille or talking books using digital technology.

TMF has funded the project titled 'Digital book production facility in Indian languages' since 2009. This will lead to the production of 4000 hours of DAISY Digital Talking Books by various DAISY Forum of India partner organizations in different parts of the country and, what is equally important, in different languages of our multi-lingual country.

To quote from a note written by Dipendra:

'Now working as the Director of the Regional Resource

Centre for the DAISY for All project in New Delhi, my every moment is involved in ideas and related projects such as:

- Development of screen reading software for Indian languages
- Content creation in local languages
- Introduction of the technology in Sri Lanka, Bangladesh, Pakistan, and Nepal as well as India. There are not only 22 languages but also a vast geographical and cultural diversity to deal with
- Research for affordable DAISY playback through subsidy schemes and development of a low cost player
- Creation of networking and common catalogue systems among innumerable small organizations who want to be a part of this digital revolution.'

It is truly awe-inspiring as one hears Dipendra speak of the immense potential which he and his colleagues are exploring. DAISY Talking Books can be played on CD players, mobile phones, computers, flash memory players such as i-Pod, etc.

Despite the leading role Dipendra has played and continues to play, he does not want DAISY with its great potential and future to become synonymous with his name, and works with a deep sense of commitment with others who share his vision. TMF is proud to be his partner in this mission.

SCORE and George Abraham

George Abraham became visually impaired after an attack of meningitis when he was not even one year old. Vineet Nayyar and I were convinced after our very first meeting with him that he was going to be an important partner. Not only does he have a winning charm and elegance about him, he exudes credibility. His brain is constantly ticking with innovative ideas to bring happiness and progress in the lives of the blind.

As you come to know George better, you learn about his amazing versatility. It is no surprise to discover that he was chosen as the best all-round student in his school, excelling alike in academics, debating, music and athletics. As in many other similar cases, he attributes his success to imaginative parental support and sensitive teachers. As an early evidence of his mental toughness, in defiance of conventional wisdom about what a visually impaired person can do—or not do—he decided to take mathematics as his subject for graduation.

George's strong communication skills enabled him to get a job with a leading advertising firm. But a visit to a school for the blind led to the shocked discovery about the pathetic state of education for the normal blind child. Like Dipendra, at great personal economic risk, he quit his advertising job and decided to devote his life to 'doing something for the blind'.

What enabled him to quickly establish links with those around the country working in the field was his passion for

George Abraham

> Blindness is not the real problem, it is the way we think. This is a realization I had when looking at my own life as a blind person for more than 50 years and through close interaction with thousands of blind persons while organizing cricket tournaments and communications skills development workshops across the country.
>
> Blind people were marginalized simply because blind people, their families and the community felt that they were incapable of looking after themselves and could not participate or contribute to the day to day goings on. I recognized the strong need to dismantle this myth.
>
> I made up my mind to launch a single stop Knowledge Resource with the object of using knowledge to not only inform but also inspire and empower the stakeholders so that the world we live in becomes a level playing field for all. I did approach a number of organizations and individuals with the intent of garnering support with little success.
>
> Tech Mahindra Foundation, the moment they heard the idea, put up their hands and decided to back it. They agreed that the blind population of the country is a huge untapped resource that needed to be invested in. I was delighted and thanks to the positive thinking and far sighted leadership and team at TMF, today Eyeway has started making a difference right across the country. Blind people have a resource to tap when in doubt for information, guidance and motivation. They have a friend who is happy to take up their issue and support they can depend upon. Thanks to TMF, today, we have managed to put up our website, broadcast a weekly radio programme that is pan India and have a helpdesk that averages close to seventy calls a week.
>
> George Abraham

cricket for the blind. Aided by a two-year fellowship from the Sir Dorabji Tata Trust, he helped organize the World Cup for the Blind in 1998 in Delhi. During this fellowship he thought through his future course of action. This led to the birth in 2002 of the website eyeway.org and an NGO which, with his love for cricket, he named SCORE (actually an acronym for Space, Contribution, Opportunity, Recognition and Equality for all). By the time George came with his proposals to TMF in 2007, he was all set to make a major countrywide impact not only with the website but a motivational radio talk beautifully entitled *Yeh Hai Roshni ka Karwan.* He has now moved on to create a TV serial, *Nazar ya Nazariya,* broadcast by Doordarshan with Naseeruddin Shah as the commentator.

A visit to SCORE's office shows the help desk busy responding to queries generated by the radio and website. In a briefing by a SCORE executive, herself a person of low vision, on the radio programme, I learn for the first time that even a visually impaired person's attendant travelling by train is entitled to a concession.

It is inspiring to hear George assert confidently that it is not necessary for the physically challenged to depend on the government for everything. He has established through his own example that much can be done by persons with disabilities themselves, assisted by their families and the community.

XRCVC and Dr Sam Taraporevala

Sam is yet another of our incredible visually impaired partners. The fact that he was blind by birth did not stand in the way of his brilliant academic record all the way to a PhD. He is now the head of the department of sociology in Mumbai's St Xavier's College, one of the country's leading colleges that also happens

George and his happy team

The XRCVC–TMF Partnership: A Reflection

Our first interaction with TMF was with Mr Vinod Khanna sometime in 2007. He had come to visit his alma mater and our meeting seemed accidental. The interaction was very exciting given the fact that he too was once upon a time a faculty at St. Xavier's. He asked many questions like any visitor to the Centre. At that time, there was no thought of partnering with TMF in our minds.

One day out of the blue, we had a call from him asking us to conceptualize a project which would synthesize the collective vision of both organizations. Given the fit between the two and our specific needs and focus areas, we worked on a project which involved building up our expertise in access technology as also support to the wider visually challenged population through the scholarship programme and our back end support.

Our relationship has grown since 2008–09 and today we are, thanks to TMF, well known across the country for our access technology, the XRCVC-Tech Mahindra Scholarship as also the wide range of support services we offer through our special educators. A recent foray this year has been in the area of creating accessible systems to promote the study of Mathematics and Science by the visually challenged.

to have a very strong tradition of social work. It is not surprising that the college administration helped Sam set-up the Xavier's Resource Centre for Visually Challenged (XRCVC).

The combination of a brilliant mind and his own experience as a blind person have helped Sam build an institution that is making most imaginative contributions to the advancement of the visually impaired community. As his generously worded tribute to TMF shows, we in TMF have been privileged to be his partners and have watched with admiration his ability to identify solutions, human, legal and technical to the various problems faced by the blind. Extremely articulate and confident, he inspires and leads lobbying efforts to persuade authorities to remove various barriers that stand in the way of the blind having a level playing field. XRCVC has played a lead role in ensuring that the visually impaired can appear in various exams on a fair and just basis. As vice president of the Daisy Forum of India and the head of its policy implementation wing, he has worked closely with Dipendra to overcome copyright hurdles standing in the way of preparing books in blind-friendly formats.

> Our relationship has been one based on mutual trust and respect and that has given the partnership a vibrancy which is finding expression in the Vision for India (VFI) initiative which likeminded organizations like ours have launched through the good offices of TMF.
>
> Thank you TMF.
>
> Dr Sam Taraporevala
> Director, XRCVC
> Associate Professor and Head,
> Department of Sociology,
> St. Xavier's College.

Sam and his team are eager to convert XRCVC into a Nodal Assistive Technology Centre. The goal is to maintain itself as a one-stop technological destination enabling a visually impaired person to make an appropriate choice. They are constantly trying out latest assistive technology that would open new vistas, ranging from talking thermometers to talking wristwatches, for the blind.

Further, Sam tells us, the same set-up can also be used as a very effective awareness centre, as a place to demonstrate the 'how' of the way visually challenged persons can effectively operate with technology. This would help sensitize key stake holders such as employers, doctors, concerned parents, educational institutions and any other concerned groups.

A meeting with Kritika, a young visually impaired girl who was helped to overcome multiple hurdles on the way to acquiring a Bachelor of Physical Therapy degree, gave an insight to the tremendous multiplier effect assistive technology can have. The daughter of an auto-rickshaw driver, she can fulfil her dream of becoming a qualified physiotherapist by using an Interferential Current Therapy talking machine.

Speaking to some of the young visually challenged persons whose lives have been transformed by the scholarships funded by TMF and implemented by XRCVC was one more gratifying and humbling experience as I moved from city to city trying to gauge

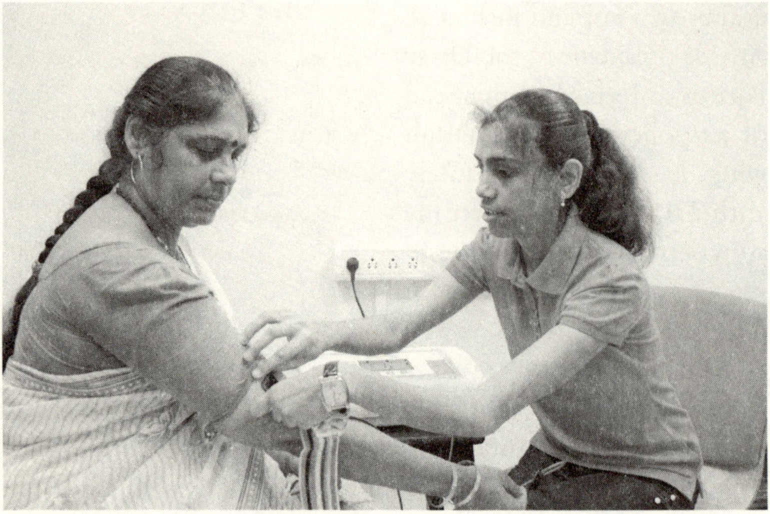

Kritika, a visually impaired physical therapist to be

the long-term impact of our Foundation's work. The XRCVC-Tech Mahindra Foundation Scholarship aims to specially support visually impaired students pursuing professional postgraduate education though it is open to other needy VI students as well. The candidate should have already secured admission in the course of their choice. The selected candidates are awarded a scholarship of up to Rs 50,000 to cover college and hostel fees as well as the cost of educational materials.

I heard with amazement the extraordinary story of a young visually impaired man who lost his father when he was two and whose mother had to eke out a living as a babysitter. The TMF scholarship enabled him to do an MBA, specializing in finance from a prestigious management school. He has gone on to become a senior manager, corporate strategy, in a reputed company. He clearly has the potential to go far. In the meanwhile, what gives him profound satisfaction is that he has been able to bring about a sea-change in his mother's life.

Equally inspiring is the story of Kailash, who lost his vision at nine. The son of a fisherman, he lives in a well-known fishing community of Mumbai.

After graduating with a degree in sociology, he was able to get a Master's in Social Work (MSW) from the renowned Tata Institute of Social Sciences (TISS) thanks to a TMF scholarship.

i) *A distant view of the fishing community which is home to Kailash, a visually impaired MSW*

ii) *Kailash at home with some of the youth whom he mentors*

One cannot but listen with wonder as he describes a typical day in his life: off in the morning to the Government Law College in Churchgate to earn a law degree, then to TISS in Chembur where he works as a coordinator, back home in Machhimar Nagar and then, after 9 p.m. act as a mentor to about twenty youths from his community in the tiny loft of his home, guiding and inspiring them on personality development. His dream is to do a PhD in some good university abroad on development issues relating to fisher folk and come back to work for his fishing community.

And there is Shilpa, who is blind from birth. With a BA degree in sociology from Delhi, she is now pursuing a MSW course at TISS in Mumbai with a TMF scholarship. The issue which concerns her deeply is child trafficking. She is determined to work for these children. Shilpa takes your breath away with her simple explanation for her career choice, 'Their situation is worse than mine; makes me forget my problems.'

Our Mumbai staff tells us of the their exciting and educative experience at the sensitization workshop organized by XRCVC. Aptly entitled Antarchakshu, the Eye Within, it takes a visitor through all the challenges which a visually challenged person goes through each and every day.

Sarthak and Dr Jitender Aggarwal

On 7 February 2012, Tech Mahindra hired five visually impaired candidates. Behind the offer letter, given by Vineet Nayyar, lay not only years of determination of these five fine young men but the vision, organizational skills and persistence of Dr Jitender Aggarwal, the founder/CEO of Sarthak Education Trust.

Jitender was a practicing dentist, married to a dentist; they were running two clinics and were parents to a three-year-old when he became a victim of macular degeneration. This destroyed his central vision. It was not possible to continue with dentistry any more. What followed was three years of 'groping in darkness', both literally and *metaphorically*. Then in 2007 he heard for the first time that the blind could operate computers. And in less than three months, he had moved from zero computer literacy to adequate competence with the help of a kind teacher.

Jitender did a survey about employment opportunities for the blind and was distressed to find that it was practically impossible for them to find a suitable job even after doing good vocational courses. And so he decided that it would be his life's mission to help the blind get decent employment. Backed by his family, he set up the Sarthak Education Trust.

It was around this time that he heard about Bangalore-based Shanti Raghavan, to whose work we shall turn shortly, and decided that she had the right model for improving the employability of the blind. He went to Bangalore and stayed there for two months to be Shanti's understudy. On return, he set up a training centre and also strove to develop contacts with potential employers. This is what first brought him to Tech Mahindra. Our conversation with him convinced us that Sarthak would be a valuable partner.

In a remarkable initiative, Jitender expanded the scope of Sarthak to cover not only the visually impaired but also the orthopaedically challenged and, even more bravely, the hearing impaired. Through a careful study of the market, Sarthak endeavours to identify precise employment opportunities for its trainees where their abilities match the required skills. To prevent a miss between the cup and the lip, Sarthak hand holds its trainees all the way up to actual employment.

With the help of TMF, Sarthak has set up an employment cell comprising of a team of dedicated staff to manage all aspects of the employment programme, ranging from networking with HR departments of prospective employers to catalyzing all processes that will assist appropriate integration of the candidate into the job.

It was not at all surprising that when the idea of Tech Mahindra SMART centres was conceptualized, Sarthak was chosen as the first such centre for the physically challenged. The centre was inaugurated by Vineet Nayyar and his wife Reva on 15 April 2013.

And this brings me to the five visually impaired young men trained by Sarthak and hired by Tech Mahindra. To quote TM's assistant manager training, Madhu, 'They have proved that capabilities and talent are not limited to physical attributes alone . . . The zeal to expand their horizons made them put in those extra inputs to make sure they were able to stand neck to neck with others.'

i) *Dr Jitender Aggarwal*

ii) *Sarthak's Tech Mahindra SMART Centre*

She goes on to inform us, 'They were shortlisted based on their work experience, computer skills and education and are hired for various corporate projects.

'Rajesh Kumar and Rashid Hassan are aligned to training; wherein their scope of work would include inducting new batches on training modality at Tech Mahindra. Arun will be a part of MIS. Hitesh Chhabra will work with the quality team and Virendra Singh is all set to explore his learning with the recruitment team. The initiative has been possible because of the confidence imbibed by the account owners/managers, Sarthak Institute and Tech Mahindra Foundation.'

It was a real pleasure meeting them a year after their recruitment and to find them all confidently settled in their respective assignments and proud to be Tech Mighties.

i) *The proud new visually challenged Tech Mighties and Madhu, their trainer*

ii) *The Tech Mighties at work*

With tremendous commitment, Sarthak organizes job fairs for the physically challenged in different parts of the country. In June 2013, for instance, it organized one in Chandigarh in which 300 candidates registered. Representatives of twelve leading companies attended and shortlisted eighty candidates for further consideration.

Jagriti and Sakina Bedi

Blind girls from poor rural families must be among the most disadvantaged members of our society. They are visually challenged, they are girls, they are poor and they come from rural areas where the awareness of a blind person's true potential is usually rather low. Jagriti, run by the National Federation of the Blind, Maharashtra, in Pune, under the leadership of Sakina Bedi, herself visually impaired, is a residential education

Sakina Bedi

programme for precisely such girls who are disadvantaged four times over. It is always a pleasure meeting this social worker. Her optimism and dedication convinces one that she can truly bring joy and light into the lives of these girls.

TMF sponsors the education of twenty-five girls as the grant-in-aid from the government of Maharashtra is totally inadequate to meet the needs of the institution. Our sponsorship covers the entire cost of educating the child, including food, clothing and health. We are also providing the salary for a computer teacher.

TMF also supports the running of a Braille book publication centre by Jagriti. Besides producing books for its own needs, it hopes to be able to get orders from outside agencies and so may eventually not need any support from us for this centre.

Shanti Raghavan and EnAble India

Shanti Raghavan is one of our earliest partners in Bangalore. An electronics engineer, she worked for Bel Labs and AT&T in the US before her passion for solutions to the problem of employability of the visually impaired was triggered by her brother losing his eyesight and his subsequent difficulties in getting a suitable job despite being an MBA topper. She returned to India and launched EnAble India (note the imaginative capitalization of 'A') in 1999 while working for GE. From 2004 onwards, it has been a full-time commitment with strong support from her equally highly qualified husband Dipesh. This non-profit organization works towards the economic independence and dignity of persons with all kinds of disabilities like visually impaired, hearing impaired, mental retardation, mental illness and more across India. To quote from its literature:

'EnAble India's mission is to empower people with disabilities. Its core activities are employment of people with disabilities, pre-employment services, supplemental education, counselling and support services, consultancy and training for other institutions and NGOs and technology services.'

Having heard about her from several people in the field, I took advantage of her visit to Delhi to invite her for a chat over a cup of tea at the India International Centre. It took me a while to catch on with her vision. It was a new field for me. Matters were not helped by the fact that she speaks at a speed which would do any Formula One driver proud! But as I got accustomed to her tempo, I was impressed by her ideas to not only empower the physically challenged but also in an important sense to 'empower' their employers.

We also thought that her technology-based work had the potential through computers and Internet to eventually be useful on a very large scale, not only pan-India but in many other countries as well. And so we decided to support her e-Vidya project. (See Box)

Initially, the project moved more slowly than we had

What TMF partnership means to EnAble India

About 3 years ago, EnAble India embarked on an ambitious venture called e-Vidya.It was to have a versatile set of products which would be in text, videos, audios or any medium required to address the development and training needs of persons with different disabilities.

TMF understood the vision and supported the initial 2 phases of e-Vidya. Their support in the early stages when EnAble India was grappling with making this vision a reality has been extremely valuable . . .

What is significant is that e-Vidya has worked across geographies and cultures and has been able to use a relatively new trainer who gains expertise via the e-Vidya material.

E-Vidya's business collateral module and peer awareness modules have started benefitting candidates when they join companies in providing awareness to the company.

This is just the beginning of the impact. The material is now being given after doing the capacity building of trainers. It is only a matter of time before the innovative methodologies of EnAble India will spread around with ease due to the availability of the e-Vidya material.

Shanti Raghavan

The amazing Shanti Raghavan and her highly supportive husband Dipesh

anticipated. We were certain that this was not due either to lethargy on her part or some intrinsic flaw in her ideas. The ideas were original and so were the multiple challenges involved in concretizing them. So we waited patiently and did not waver in our support. Results have eventually started flowing in. I was delighted that we were able to release the following modules when we met to launch the Vision for India network (to which Sam made reference and on which we shall have more to say later in the chapter) in February 2012:

1. Employability Modules for Skilled/Semi Skilled Jobs for Hearing Impaired and Physically Disabled (e-learning flash)
2. Employability Guide for Skilled Jobs for Visually Impaired
3. English Manual for Visually Impaired
4. Spelling Tool for Visually Impaired
5. Work Ethics Audios for Visually Impaired and Physically Disabled

Along the way we have learnt much. We were particularly struck by Shanti's detailed understanding of how the visually impaired would negotiate their way at the work place, both physically and psychologically. We learnt from her how well-meaning bosses and fellow-workers could bend excessively backwards in adjusting to what they perceived to be the disabilities of their blind colleagues, paradoxically preventing the latter from rising to their true potential which often required only a few sensible adjustments. There is profound but understated compassion underlying EnAble India's work. This is no maudlin sentimentality. Indeed, the most rigorous demands are made of persons with disability who have to earn—and make progress in—employment by virtue of their ability and not as a matter of charity.

Shanti travels all over the country, tutoring trainers, educating employers, inspiring the physically challenged and, not surprisingly, being showered with all kinds of awards along the way.

National Association for the Blind (NAB)

NAB is perhaps India's largest voluntary organization for the blind. Among the large number of projects which the Delhi branch runs is a programme to ensure quality education for visually challenged children through integration in mainstream schools. NAB provides strong after-school support to these children. TMF has been supporting more than sixty children at NAB so they are able to receive quality education in schools like DPS R.K. Puram, Kendriya Vidyalayas, DAV and Mt Carmel where they study with normal children.

We have been most encouraged by their academic performance. Take for instance the results of the 2011 CBSE board examinations. Every child passed. All the sixteen who sat for the class twelve exam secured first division! One student secured 94 per cent and another 90 per cent. Two students were honoured with the Indira Award for their excellent performance in the board examinations.

In DAV school

Many students have done well in extracurricular activities as well and received medals in chess, athletics and cricket at different sports meets.

After school, a majority go on to pursue higher education degrees in various colleges of Delhi University. Some prefer to start working while studying by correspondence. The fact that they have had training in the excellent computer lab in NAB helps in getting reasonably paid jobs.

In fact, TMF is also supporting NAB's technology training programme. During our work with the visually challenged we have been repeatedly awestruck by the potential of the revolutionary transformation computers: it opens up new disciplines of education, increases employability, and indeed gives all the independence that reading and writing makes possible.

Bharati, herself visually impaired,
training girls including Hema who is a student
we supported in DAV

L.V. Prasad Eye Institute, Hyderabad

The L.V. Prasad Eye Institute (LVPEI), a prestigious comprehensive eye health facility with its main campus located in Hyderabad, is headed by a well-known ophthalmic surgeon Dr G.N. Rao. A World Health Organization Collaborating Centre for Prevention of Blindness, the institute offers comprehensive patient care, sight enhancement and rehabilitation services and high-impact rural eye health programmes. It also pursues cutting edge research and offers training in human resources for all levels of ophthalmic personnel.

V.C. Kumar, who was executive head of the Mahindra Satyam Foundation before it merged with TMF, informed us about the possibility of partnering LVPEI in two rather promising programmes: one is an early intervention programme that would provide individualized teaching and training services for visually impaired children between 0–8 years of age. The services include early identification of developmental delays,

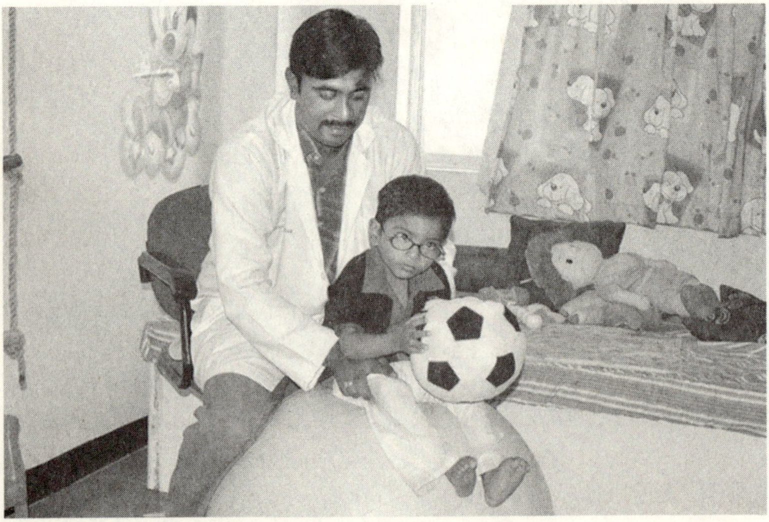

Early intervention programme

individualized and parental training, provision of devices, and follow-up services. The second one is an IT based vocational programme for the visually impaired. Given the reputation of LVPEI, we had no hesitation in agreeing. About 750 children a year are expected to benefit from the first programme and 180 youth from the latter.

Both the centres were inaugurated in November 2011, an event that was given wide publicity by the media.

Vision for India (VFI)

As the number of our partners working with the visually impaired grew, TMF and some of the NGOs felt it would be a good idea to set up a platform where they could come together to exchange ideas and where possible work together. Given the wide range of skills that they brought to their work, there was obvious scope for synergy to enrich their contribution to the field. Much brain-storming co-ordinated by our senior executive Nikhil led to the birth in February 2012 of the network named Vision for India to which some of our partners have referred in the course of this chapter.

All our partners share common goals for the visually challenged: personal independence, economic self-reliance and social inclusion for people with vision impairment. This will involve collaboration and sharing of the present expertise amongst our partners, identification of gaps in the domain and development of practical, meaningful solutions.

It is hoped that the Project VFI will gradually grow into a resource centre with a collection of several supported programmes well connected with each other.

Issues which will be addressed by this Forum are education, awareness, advocacy, technology and economic independence.

13

Initiatives for Physical Disabilities Other Than Visual Impairment

While TMF can take justifiable pride at having carved out a significant niche for itself as far as empowering the visually challenged is concerned, its support to organizations working with persons with other physical disabilities has also been fairly substantial. Sometimes, workers in this field use the acronym PWD for persons with disability—it can confuse those who are accustomed to its usage as an abbreviation for the Public Works Department! Actually, there is continuous quest for terminology that is both accurate and sensitive. Many today, for instance, prefer the term 'differently abled'.

As in the case of the visually impaired, here too we have supported programmes which extend from primary school education to life skills and livelihood. Statistics about the educational status of children with special needs in India are alarming. It appears that while the national percentage of children enrolled now has gone up to an impressive figure of over 90 per cent, less than 5 per cent of children with disabilities are enrolled in schools. The fact that about 20 million children suffer from an impairment requiring special attention at the school level—locomotor, visual, mental, speech, hearing—gives some idea of the magnitude of the problem in the country.

Suhrud, Pune

At a partners' meet in Delhi, a leading figure from an organization working for the blind who was himself visually impaired surprised the audience by saying, 'We the blind are more lucky than the hearing impaired.' Our partnership over the last five years with Suhrud in Pune has given us a vivid insight into the unique challenges involved in educating deaf and dumb children, especially if they are from economically disadvantaged families.

Suhrud Mandal works for the educational and vocational rehabilitation of children with hearing and speech impairment. Currently, there are 400 children enrolled in four different special schools of Suhrud Mandal. TMF has been supporting one of these Badhir Mook Vidyalayas (BMV) for the last five years. This has covered the purchase of hearing and sports equipment as well as education kits. We have also supported a speech therapist. To see the latter in action gives some idea of the monumental patience required to train a child deaf from birth to articulate the most basic of sounds.

On 27 August 2012, I was invited to distribute certificates and prizes to students of the school we support. This was on the basis of their performance in the Secondary School Certificate examination. It was such joy to meet the successful students, their eyes sparkling with pride, and their even prouder parents and guardians. It was particularly gratifying to meet some ex-students who are now on the way to meaningful careers. Among them were some who were talented artists and were now doing computer-based graphic design, confidently hoping to become commercial artists.

And there was this girl Kiran Kamble, who excels as a photographer and looks forward to becoming a professional with a shop of her own. She is currently doing a diploma in photography from an ITI. Her father is an auto-rickshaw driver.

Kiran: hearing impaired, but determined to be a professional photographer

Eager to support his daughter's aspiration, he took a loan of Rs 35,000 to buy her a quality camera.

Report for Tech Mahindra Foundation

Suhrud Mandal is an NGO dedicatedly working since 1973 for education and vocational rehabilitation of children with hearing impairment. Suhrud Mandal has 3 day schools, 1 residential school and 1 technical school in and around Pune. Currently, nearly 450 children are receiving education in various classes. These schools do receive salary grant from the Govt of Maharashtra, but that has significant limitations. Naturally we depend on philanthropic work of various Foundations. Tech Mahindra Foundation has a major and long-standing contribution in the shaping of Suhrud Mandal's various activities.

It all started with the support to our Chinchwad school in the year 2007. This is the only school in this area for hearing impaired children, and we wanted to upgrade the school from Class VII to Class X as parents were requesting it for

Association for People with Disability (APD), Bangalore

APD was founded more than half a century ago by N.C. Hema, wheelchair bound after a polio attack when she was five years old. She makes no secret of her disdain for the inadequate and all too often corruption-ridden government measures to help the physically challenged. She has not allowed her own disability or society's ignorance-based prejudices to come in the way of building,

> a long time. Govt of Maharashtra was reluctant to support financially. It was TMF which helped us generously with the salaries of teachers, and speech therapist. It also extended help for academic and other requirements of all the students. This helped the school tremendously. We are proud that we not only succeeded in upgrading the school upto 10th grade but got 100% result from the first batch that appeared for the S.S.C Board examination since the year 2009. So far 50 hearing impaired students have graduated with flying colours. We sincerely thank TMF for this generous support.
>
> Last year, TMF indicated to us to have a paradigm shift and recommended that the focus should be on vocational rehabilitation of hearing impaired children. With this in mind we started a DTP course at our Vocational Training Centre and also IBT (Introduction to Basic Technology) for students of VIII, IX and X class based on the philosophy of Vigyan Ashram, Pabal, Dist. Pune.
>
> Abhaya Wadikar,
> Hon. Secretary, Suhrud Mandal

with the help of a very fine team, an amazing institution that reaches out to a very wide range of disabilities—locomotor disability, speech and hearing impairment, cerebral palsy, multiple and severe disability (either congenital or a result of spinal-cord injury). It caters holistically to the needs of the disabled covering academics, occupational-skill teaching, and, yes, play. For APD, the aim is very clear: to offer comprehensive rehabilitation to the disabled and help integrate them into the mainstream as effectively as possible. All their programmes are geared towards making the disabled self-reliant and independent so they can lead a life of self-esteem and dignity.

Sharing TMF's philosophy, APD considers education a crucial input towards development and inclusion of children with disability into mainstream human activities. Therefore, TMF has been happy to support APD's Shradhanjali Integrated School (SIS). This is a recognized primary school from nursery to class eight, following the state board curriculum and has the capacity to educate 185 children. To promote inclusion, 80 per cent of the students are disabled. Most of the children come from poor families. The school aims at preparing these children for the next higher class in mainstream schools. Contributing to all round development are co-curricular activities like sports, cultural festivals, and arts and crafts as in any good school. To meet the special needs of their children, an integral part of the programme is medical rehabilitation, ensured through regular medical check-ups, physiotherapy and use of mobility aids.

One marvels at the versatility of the teachers of SIS as one class has students with different disabilities. Clearly, the teachers have had excellent training. Particularly impressive are the imaginative methods used for teaching children with cerebral palsy.

With the help of contributions from donors like TMF, APD has established a well-equipped computer lab with appropriate CDs that are used to teach children with various disabilities, especially those who have communication and writing issues.

Our Bangalore manager Mamatha testifies to the veracity of APD's claim that detailed and careful planning and coordination between teachers, speech therapist and volunteers are the key success factors of SIS.

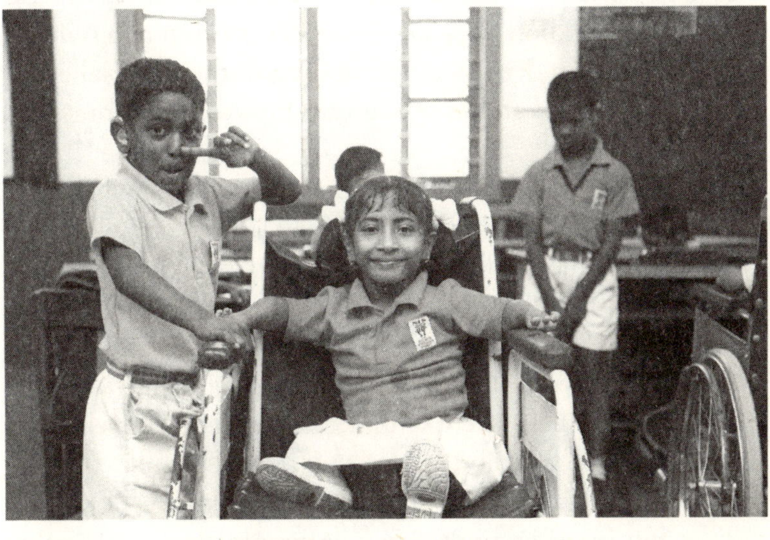

Happy learners despite various disabilities

All too often when we encounter a victim of cerebral palsy we make all sorts of ignorance-cum-pity based assumptions about their future. Indeed, in the absence of institutions like APD we may not be altogether wrong. But some time spent in Shraddhanjali Integrated School comes as a most welcome eye-opener. APD has every reason to speak with pride about students like Mohammad Waquas who joined the school in the fourth standard in 2002. He could neither speak nor write. Cerebral palsy had led to multiple disabilities. But APD teachers soon identified him as a very bright and intelligent child. With the help of the Alternative Augmentative Communication Chart, his academic learning progressed gradually. He learnt to type and did all his assignments and tests on the computer. When we met him, Mohammed was in the ninth in a mainstream school where teachers were oriented and trained by APD on his special needs and was progressing well.

An important element of SIS's philosophy is its training to the parents of these special children. The parents are regarded as 'key partners of SIS'. They are given information and training so they develop a deeper understanding of their special child; this also ensures seamless continuity between the home and the school.

While I have visited APD many times and have had detailed discussions with its management and faculty, it was only when I sat down to talk to the children and their parents that I realized the full magnitude of the achievement of all those involved: the institution, the parent and above all the child. One comes away confident that these young people will be able to lead a life of dignity and self-reliance with the help of TMF-funded programmes implemented with intelligence, skill and compassion by APD.

Continuous interaction of our manager with APD led to partnership in an important new initiative. Recognizing that all too often precious years are wasted before an affected

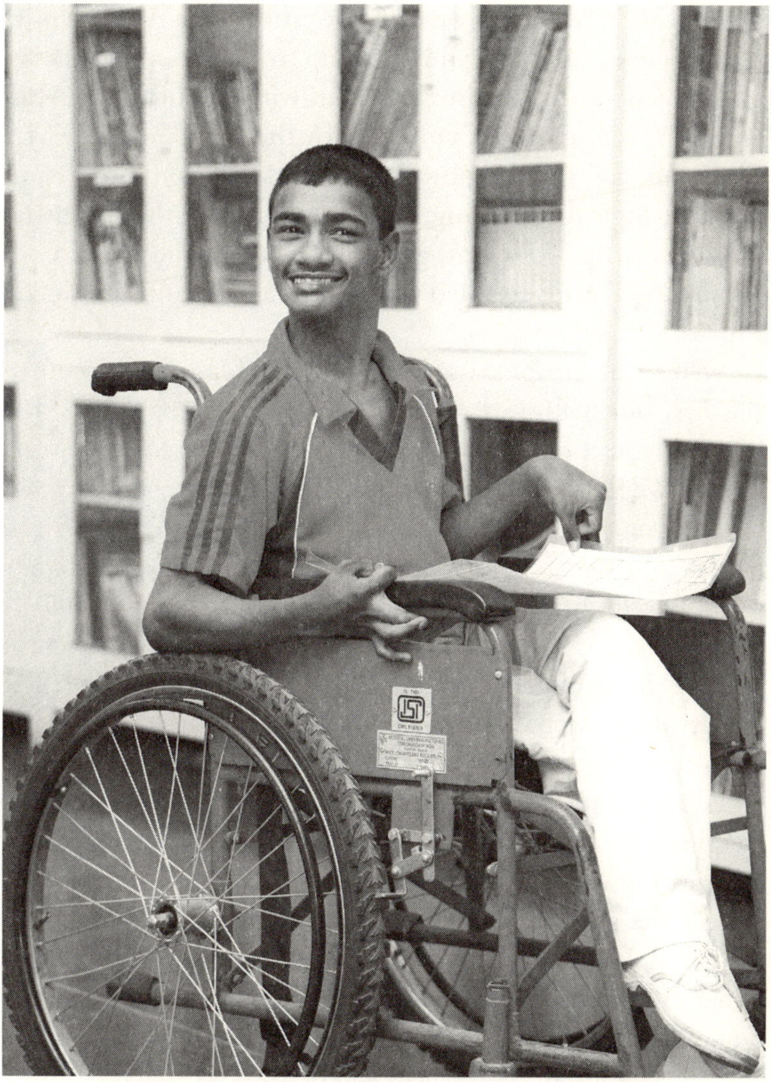

'No disability can rob me of my Right to Education'

impoverished family realizes the nature of their special child's problem and what can be done about it, SIS has developed, with TMF's help, an early detection and intervention programme.

Another new area of our collaboration with APD is in its impressive vocational training set-up to ensure employability of disabled youth. To provide them with a solid start, APD now runs a foundation course with the assistance of TMF. This aims at ensuring appropriate life skills, communication English, logical reasoning, basic maths and other essential trainings. To make the programme inclusive and integrated, 20 per cent non-disabled youth are also admitted to the course.

When the proposal relating to the foundation course was first put before us, we were not entirely convinced that it would be a cost-effective use of our limited resources. Today, we have no such doubts. Take, for instance, the case of a sixteen-year-old girl who is from an impoverished rural family and has a speech and hearing impairment. Thanks to APD's foundation course, she has picked up sufficient communication skills based on sign language and Yuva English to have the confidence to one day get a job and support her family after she has further enhanced her employability by learning to operate computers.

Equally inspiring is the story of another village girl, the daughter of a daily wage labourer, who also suffers from speech and hearing impairment. During her studies in the foundation course, she got interested in IT and wanted to pursue higher studies in computers. After proper counselling and assessment of her capacity, she was supported to get admission in a graphic designing course run by APD. She is confident that she will be able to get a job in the IT field and become self-reliant.

Some of those finishing the foundation course have been able to join a course leading to a diploma in computer science in JSS College, Mysore one of the very few colleges training speech and hearing impaired candidates.

APD-run TMF-funded foundation course will ensure our future

Amar Jyoti

Dr Uma Tuli was awarded Padma Shri in 2012 for her work in the field of inclusive education through Amar Jyoti, the NGO founded by her. She has been our partner from long before she received this richly deserved recognition. Amar Jyoti is a voluntary organization providing comprehensive rehabilitative services to persons with disabilities through integrated education, medical care, vocational training etc. To promote inclusive education, Amar Jyoti runs a school where over 450 children with and without disability are studying together in equal numbers.

Amar Jyoti has several features one does not find in a normal institution devoted to the education of children with special needs. It has a whole range of in-house facilities which enables it to offer holistic inclusive education. It has a prosthetic and orthotic unit which can provide children appropriate artificial limbs, calipers and other aids to improve or restore their mobility. It is also in a position to offer healthcare services through its OPD wing which offers free consultations in different specialties like medical, surgical, orthopaedic, eye, ENT, paediatrics and speech therapy.

Much effort is devoted to addressing the special needs of each child and devising a pedagogic approach appropriate to her/his impairment. The curriculum and examination system is suitably modified. A crucial role is played by counsellors whose services are available to deal with academic, social, emotional, behavioural or mental health concerns. Naturally, given the fact that the school has speech and hearing impaired children, it has speech therapists. But they also have other rehabilitation professionals such as occupational therapists and physiotherapists.

As is our normal practice, we had an intensive interaction with Dr Tuli to make an objective assessment of the needs of Amar Jyoti. We began by sponsoring the education of a

The English language lab

hundred children but gradually expanded our cooperation to further enrich the education being offered by the school. Over the years, this has included providing an English language lab and support to the science and computer labs. Each visit to the school reveals encouraging evidence of the additional value these have brought to the learning levels of the children. Gradually, English communication skills are increasing. We were happy to learn that the school has been able to hold its first elocution and debating contests in English.

A visit to the science lab shows significant improvement in children's conceptual learning.

As in any good school, Amar Jyoti's auditorium often comes alive with music and dance. Some years ago, the children of this remarkable institution gave a spectacular display at a Republic Day parade. Their annual days are delightfully colourful events. It was thrilling to see how Dr Tuli and her team have nurtured the abilities of the differently abled children under their care

An essential feature of inclusive education

Amar Jyoti has always encouraged its physically challenged children to participate in sports. I saw, for instance, a fine exhibition of archery by an orthopaedically challenged boy. A particular source of joy was an inter-school sports event organized by Amar Jyoti and sponsored by TMF.

The laughter and excitement of the children validated Dr Tuli's statement: 'The main achievement of our partnership is a smile on every child's face in school.'

Jan Madhyam

In general, TMF has not undertaken to support programmes for mentally challenged children primarily because we just do not have the requisite knowhow to assess them. Only three of our partners work in this area. Some children being catered to by APD's Shraddhanjali school in Bangalore and Amar Jyoti in Delhi fall in this category. The third is Jan Madhyam which works in a semi-rural part of Delhi through its programme

Inter-school sports meet sponsored by TMF, organized by Amar Jyoti

titled Equal Opportunity Rural Training and Education Center (EORTEC, for marginalized and disabled children and young adults). Jan Madhyam has brought a sense of hope in the life of girls who suffer from multiple challenges: intellectual, economic, social. It has taught them simple vocations and life skills to make them self reliant. The group has imaginatively used music, dance, painting, clay work, games and puppetry to provide a platform for creative expression. Any visitor to the centre in Ayanagar cannot but be amazed at the confidence and dignity with which these girls conduct themselves.

One of our most exciting partnerships in the field of the physically challenged is with Anandwan, founded by that legendary figure, Baba Amte. The next chapter is devoted to this unique organization.

14

Anandwan: A Very Special Partner

For anybody who has ever dreamt of doing something seemingly impossible for the good of any suffering section of humanity, Anandwan stands as a beacon of hope. It is a unique community, born of the vision and almost superhuman compassion of one of independent India's most amazing personalities, Baba Amte. Quite simply put, it is a pilgrimage spot to which one goes with curiosity and returns humbled but energized about taking up new challenges on behalf of those less fortunate.

Baba Amte's work for lepers is well-known but only in very general terms. The fact that his work went well beyond lepers is known only to very few. It was the very powerful advocacy of Milind Kulkarni, who has been one of the major pillars of the Tech Mahindra Foundation from its very birth, which led us to take a closer look at what is happening in Anandwan.

Baba Amte had acquired, even as a young man, the reputation of being a fearless fighter for just causes. Gandhiji called him an 'Abhay Sadhak'. But his life work began when he encountered a badly disfigured leper. His initial reaction was of fear and revulsion. Disturbed by his unexpected show of cowardice he took up the challenge to work for lepers.

> 'Work builds, charity destroys'
> —Baba Amte

Having decided to devote his life to the service of those

struck by leprosy, he took a crash course in leprosy treatment, and established an organization called Maharogi Sewa Samiti (MSS) in 1949. For the lepers, often abandoned by their indigent and ill-informed families, despised and stigmatized by an equally ignorant society, he created Anandwan, the Forest of Joy, on fifty acres of wasteland gifted by the state government in Warora, some 100 kilometres from Nagpur.

While medical facilities were gradually established to cure the victims of leprosy, Baba Amte knew that even those cured would not be welcomed back and so he had a unique concept for Anandwan. It was a residential commune of those cured of leprosy. His motto was: give them a chance and not charity. The essence of Anandwan was captured by Acharya Vinoba Bhave when he inaugurated it in June 1951: 'Its name Anandwan is most appropriate. You have created happiness in life through work. You have discarded the begging bowl in exchange for honest labour, recognizing its inherent divinity.' Baba was a disciple alike of Gandhi, Tagore and Ambedkar, but a genuine charismatic figure in his own right.

Gradually, Anandwan extended its support, with its trademark blend of imagination and love, to other marginalized and suffering, including those suffering from various physical disabilities. In all cases, the goal was a life of dignity and self-reliance.

Baba Amte passed away in February 2008. TMF's partnership with MSS began a few months later when, inspired by Milind's reports, we started assisting in a small way the two residential schools for special children, one for the blind and the other for deaf and dumb children.

MSS does not turn back any affected child. And so it has more children than covered by the rather inadequate government grants. We decided to sponsor the seventy additional children.

They all come from poor rural families. Our support covers boarding, accommodation and educational expenses.

Baba Amte and the Anandwan children

TMF supports both sports and studies in Anandwan

Our dialogue with MSS has grown steadily. Our Pune-based executive Vijay and later Nikhil Pant from Delhi visited Anandwan. We discovered that despite its international reputation, MSS was constantly faced with serious financial shortages for even the most obvious needs. And so the range of our partnership expanded to provide nutritional support to the children in response to a carefully argued case by Baba Amte's granddaughter Dr Sheetal Amte who worked out a sensible cost-effective programme for supplementing the nutritional content of the food that MSS was providing in these two schools. These children come from economically challenged families in remote areas of Maharashtra with rampant malnourishment. Even though TMF generally does not enter the field of health, it agreed with Sheetal's plea that besides a whole range of other medical problems, 'malnutrition reduces attention span in schools which further impacts their scholastic performance and overall receptivity'.

It was so heart-warming a few months later to receive the following message from Sheetal:

'We have successfully launched the scheme, "Provision of nutritious breakfast to children in special schools" from July 17th . . . Whenever I go for a walk in the evening, they all surround me and give a detailed account of their day that starts with a fantastic breakfast. The smile on their faces is a true realization of Baba's philosophy, "The smile of a man who is oppressed or a child who is suffering is what I covet more than any award".'

TMF's support has extended to cover several other areas such as sports, music and crafts that go on to define holistic education. With qualified coaches and appropriate equipment funded by TMF, the children, be they boys or girls, visually or hearing impaired, are all able to play various games, as is the entitlement of every child.

Music has an important role to play in any sensibly run school programme; and for blind children it is absolutely critical. Painting seems to play the same role for the hearing and speech impaired. These arts dramatically brighten the lives of these children. A visit to the music class for the blind and arts class for the hearing and speech impaired brings fresh realization of how nature compensates by investing these children with extra talents denied to an average 'normal' child. Guided by a teacher who is himself an artist, the speech and hearing impaired create beautiful paintings. In the crafts class, one can see girls knit beautiful woollens. Anandwan is even able to sell some.

One of the great joys of a visit to Anandwan is the opportunity to attend a performance by this community's unique orchestra, the Swaranandwan. It has more than 200 members, including the leprosy afflicted and vision, speech and hearing impaired and other physically challenged. I was privileged to see a very large proportion of them display their talents on the stage. Particularly fascinating was the performance of deaf children . . . it appeared that they were dancing to the beat of music, as if they were not deaf at all, a tribute alike to those who have trained them and their own hard work.

At the performance I was introduced to one of Anandwan's famous personalities, Sadashiv Tajne. The wheelchair bound Sadashiv, yet another victim of a childhood attack of polio, is the chief coordinator of Swaranandwan and organizes its programmes and tours. Apparently, when he was young he had no access to a wheelchair and would cover the long distances to school and college with his slippers in hand!

Sadashiv has also been a main figure in the evolution of Anandwan's vocational training institute, called Sandhiniketan, the Home of Opportunities, which TMF has now started supporting. He was the first student when it was inaugurated in 1972. Sandhiniketan provides training in a variety of trades such as tailoring, electrical work, handicrafts, carpet weaving

A trainee at Anandwan's vocational training institute

and leather work. The trainees at Sandhiniketan are the cured leprosy patients as well as physically handicapped youth. Once trained, they are encouraged to go back to their families and earn a livelihood. But those who are not accepted by society are rehabilitated either in the running of Anandwan itself or in one of the several production centres of Anandwan. Their output is sold to generate income. A visit to the shop in Anandwan gives an idea of the range and quality of their products.

Today, Baba Amte's family carries on his legacy. One listens with fascination to Dr Vikas Amte, Baba's elder son, who is secretary of MSS (Dr Prakash Amte, the younger son, manages Hemalkasa Project, which is located in Naxal-infected Gadchiroli districts and focuses on medical aid and education) as he spoke of Baba's vision. Modestly he had little to say about the comprehensive role he himself has played in taking Anandwan to where it is today.

The responsibility for taking Anandwan ahead is falling on the third generation. Baba's grandson Kaustubh, a chartered accountant, brings to the running of this now huge institution his management skills. Beginning with Baba's wife, the redoubtable Sadhana Tai, women of the family have been as active as the men folk. Indeed, as far as the projects being supported by TMF, the two schools, are concerned, our main interface is with Baba's granddaughter, Sheetal, a doctor. One is profoundly impressed by her dedication, her compassion and her eagerness to learn.

It is never easy to carry forward the legacy of a world-renowned charismatic figure. The members of the three generations of the Amte family may not all have identical views and with changing times new ideas will no doubt emerge. But what is common to all of them is an unwavering commitment to creating an

Sheetal and her father, Dr Vikas Amte

empowered and dignified life for all those suffering from some painful affliction or the other who come to Anandwan for solace, succour and above all hope. To this noble endeavour, TMF is a modest contributor.

15

Volunteering for Good Causes

The top leadership of the Mahindra Group has always encouraged its personnel to volunteer some of their time to good causes. This comes through clearly in any conversation with Keshub Mahindra, Anand Mahindra, Vineet Nayyar or C.P. Gurnani (popularly known as CP), Managing Director and CEO, Tech Mahindra. To quote from a powerful plea addressed by Vineet to all his colleagues in the company:

'We have been doing splendid work through the Foundation and continue to do so. But is that enough? I firmly believe that true CSR in a corporate goes far beyond the signing of the cheque. I believe it comes with every individual in the organization believing in the cause we support. It comes with each one of us complementing and contributing to the cause. It comes with all of us unanimously wanting to make a difference to that cause.

'And I write this mail to you to invite you to be part of a movement that can bring about that difference.'

Fortunately, Satyam also had a strong tradition of volunteering. To cite just one example, when we took over the management of Satyam Foundation, we were particularly impressed by the concept of 'Magnificent Seven' under which a certain number of Satyam employees would constitute themselves into groups of seven. Each of these would adopt a government school and undertake to teach in it every Saturday. They would not only pool their collective skills to respond to the needs of the children but also ensure that continuity was not disturbed if on any Saturday if one or more of the volunteers could not make it.

TMF has given TM associates an opportunity to volunteer in any NGO it is supporting at any given time. Their participation has been rising steadily. In mid-2011, the TMF team developed a TMF-Volunteering Programme that enables TechMighties to be involved in CSR work that it carries out. All NGO partners were asked to identify the kind of work a volunteer could do in their organization. The idea was that it should not be mere window-dressing exercise but a contribution as added value to their work. This information has been shared with TM associates. Volunteering can be done either through sharing one's physical time or through e-volunteering from a distance or both for a cause close to their heart.

Tech Mahindra volunteer teachers

Naturally some of the most significant contributions made by our volunteers are those that have involved use of their special skills for the benefit of the disadvantaged. Take for instance, a three-month initiative to bridge the digital divide where senior Tech Mahindra associates provided basic computer training to NGO functionaries in Tech Mahindra's office in Sharda, Pune, every Sunday. This has been translated into a handbook—A Resource Manual—for scaling/replication in other locations.

In the chapter on our work with the visually impaired, we spoke of TMF's support to the project, 'Digital book production facility in Indian languages' being run by Saksham Trust which works as the secretariat for DAISY Forum of India. Many volunteers from Tech Mahindra have volunteered time to do recordings for DAISY books. More important was the response to Daisy Foundation's request to prepare a training module for 'OBI Tool' widely used for preparing 'digital talking books'. A team from TM accepted this challenge to produce this before the Global Daisy Workshop scheduled at Delhi on 28–29 October 2010, where this was to be formally launched. The product was made ready a month before the scheduled date.

Another volunteer has worked on developing a tool to teach or practice keyboard with audio feedback for the Saksham Trust.

Vidya and Child has a TechMighty helping it to develop a web-based application which can access the database of the after-school support programme.

Naturally, many of our volunteers coming as they do from a science background have been able to help high school children in subjects like maths and physics.

In the chapter on women empowerment, I described the exciting Bangalore-based scholarship programme Katalyst run for brilliant girls from economically difficult backgrounds. Our volunteers have expressed readiness to mentor some of them.

Another much needed skill has been English language. Many of our volunteers have helped out in the English language component of some vocational training programmes implemented by our NGO partners.

Hundreds of TM personnel associate themselves through NGOs with activities such as donation of books and toys and organizing of festivals.

I referred earlier to the fact that the work of our partner India Sponsorship Committee (ISC) with the children of brick kiln workers is not too far from TM's Hinjewadi campus. This proximity has facilitated valuable volunteering by a group of TechMighties. ISC personnel expressed great appreciation of our volunteers helping their staff by taking classes on spoken English and basic computer education. Similarly, the relative proximity of Door Step School's study centre to our Sharda centre office has encouraged a group of TM volunteers to volunteer teaching and mentoring of their students.

One of our Mumbai-based volunteers has helped the SPRJK Trust with data management work.

While putting finishing touches to the book, I received the following encouraging report about volunteering from TMF's team in Pune:

1. The associates from the Business Support Group (BSG) have taken the responsibility of conducting special soft skill sessions at the Tech Mahindra SMART centre Yerwada. The centre gives vocational training to underprivileged youth in computers, English and work readiness and BSG associates visit them every Saturday to interact and help them get work-ready through intensive soft skill sessions.
2. A few associates are scanning and editing the tenth standard science guide which will then be converted into Braille for visually impaired students. This is done by volunteers from

home and we are hoping to involve many more associates in this project.

3. Associates have come forward to form volunteering teams that adopt a project and make sure that there is sustained volunteering done. Thus, every Saturday, two associates from Team Crusaders go to the Door Step study centre and explain scientific principles through simple experiments. The Door Step study centre attracts the children from the surrounding slums who want a place to study and access to educational materials and help in learning.
4. Associates came together to help out the drought affected villages of Maharashtra. They not only contributed to the relief fund to help out the villages of Purandar and Sangola taluka but also enthusiastically volunteered their time to help the needy in these villages. The last few months has seen the volunteers visit villages, join hands with the villagers and doing work at the grassroot level—digging water pits, trenches, planting trees etc. About 120 TechMighties with thirteen family members made five visits over three months to put in more than 750 hours of work in these villages.

Our Bangalore team reported that our volunteers have visited Parikrma Learning Centre and worked out a plan of action on what they can do best for the children. The team would now meet on a regular basis and carry out various volunteering activities.

Another favourite activity of volunteers is running in the Airtel Delhi Half Marathons for one or the other of our NGO partners.

Actually, at Tech Mahindra, the Foundation is not the only platform available to its associates to make voluntary contributions to the needy. There is, for instance, an organization of associates aptly named Josh which sponsors a wide range of activities, including entertainment related and blood donation camps.

C.P. Gurnani

Volunteers, helping to make a difference in the lives of those they have the privilege to serve, invariably speak of the good it does to *them*. They derive profound happiness by being able to help somebody who needs their time or skills. In many cases, they have spoken of the sheer joy experienced by them when some elementary act by them has brought a beautiful smile on the face of person less fortunate than them in life. Quite simply, it makes them feel that in some important way they have become better human beings.

Tech Mahindra Managing Director CP captures the driving spirit behind volunteering, 'I have been touched by the passion, perseverance and purpose shown by many of you towards volunteering. Do continue the good work.'

16

EMRI and HMRI: Saving Lives

There is one incredibly important contribution being made by Tech Mahindra to the well-being of hundreds of thousands in the country. Though not administered by the Foundation, and not falling within its present agenda, it is a striking manifestation of the company's sense of social responsibility and so deserves mention in this book.

This is not the place to trace the dramatic events that led to the acquisition of Satyam by Tech Mahindra and the ultimate merger of Mahindra Satyam into Tech Mahindra. Along the way, Tech Mahindra has inherited a critical role in the running of EMRI, the GVK Emergency Management and Research Institute. At the heart of the justly renowned '108' emergency call service is technology, and that has been delivered uninterruptedly, pro bono, by the Satyam–Mahindra Satyam–Tech Mahindra continuum in the midst of all the corporate upheavals. In a message to GVK EMRI, Anand Mahindra, had this to say, '. . . We can together be genuinely proud of pioneering an innovation, scaling it at a very rapid pace and managing it very efficiently to service a very critical need for human kind.' To this, C.P. Gurnani adds, 'GVK EMRI is a unique service, focused just on one thing—saving a life in danger . . . So each time someone in distress refers to 108 as a "miracle" we at Mahinda Satyam feel proud to have essayed an important role behind it.' These messages by Anand and CP antedate the merger of Mahindra Satyam into Tech Mahindra which has, of course, continued this invaluable partnership.

At the latest count, some 6,50,000 lives have been saved by EMRI, and the institute is moving rapidly towards its vision of saving a million lives annually while responding to 30 million emergencies.

As the technology partner of GVK EMRI, we have been associated with the development, maintenance and upgradation of the centralized automated emergency management system which integrates all the key functions of taking the call, defining the problem, coordinating the response and providing emergency care.

Today, Tech Mahindra has a sixty-two-member team dedicated to the maintenance and upgradation of this technology-driven system. Siddhartha Bhattacharya, chief operating officer (AP) and National Integrator Technology & Marketing of GVK EMRI, elucidated this for us. He pointed out, in his briefing to us, that technology plays a critical role in ensuring *timely* response

i) *EMRI ambulances lined up for action.*
Photo courtesy GVK EMRI

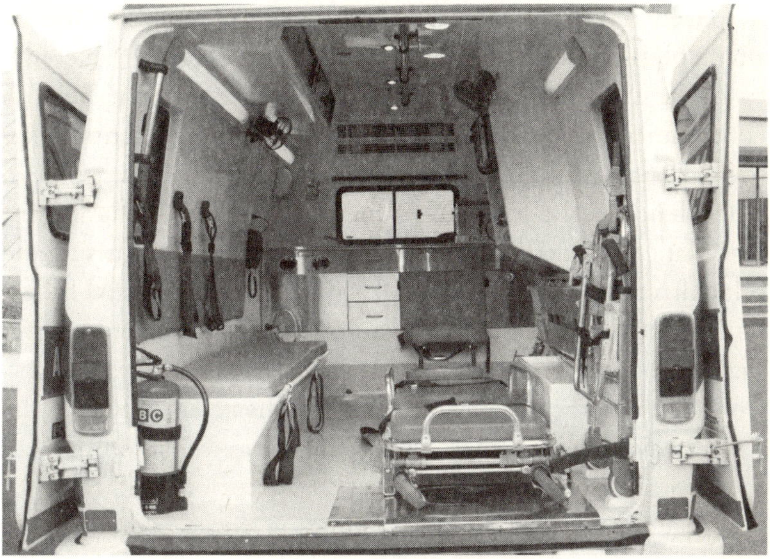

ii) *Inside an '108' ambulance. Photo courtesy GVK EMRI*

by the available resources which huge though they may appear to be—there are, for instance, about 6000 ambulances—are relatively limited when compared to the scale of the operations.

It is one of the most successful not-for profit public-private partnerships. The ultimate ownership rests with the state governments. The relationship works efficiently and without the governance bottlenecks for which the political–bureaucratic nexus is so notorious. No matter which party runs a state government, it is happy to be associated with this highly visible life-saving programme. Indeed, the souvenir brought out by GVK EMRI on completion of seven years of its service, was studded with glowing tributes from chief ministers cutting across party divides. The GVK EMRI agreements with state governments contains the provision that the licence for the Emergency Response Applications Suite will be provided free by Tech Mahindra.

Based on the TM-maintained technology platform, a single phone call to 108 sets in motion a process which comes to the rescue of those in desperate need of urgent help. A communication officer at the emergency response centre takes the call, passes the relevant information to a dispatch officer, who identifies the location of the emergency and the nearest ambulance. Immediately, the ambulance team, comprising the pilot/driver and the emergency medical technician (EMT), are sent to the rescue, determined to provide essential emergency care within the golden hour. Taking instructions where necessary from the emergency response centre physician (ERCP), the EMT provides emergency care on the site as well as on the way to the nearest health centre.

There is a continuous flow of amazing stories from different parts of the country of the efficiency, skill and commitment with which GVK EMRI team keeps saving lives.

Emergency Response Centre. Photo courtesy GVK EMRI

Here's a story that comes from Assam. On 28 March 2013 at 2.45 p.m., a call was received about a road accident in the Padmabill area of the Kokrajhar district. On arrival at the site, EMT Kamal Kumar and pilot Sujit Kumar found that the car was surrounded by a hundred odd people looking on helplessly. Two men were badly trapped in the wreckage. The 108 team carefully extricated both the victims, one bleeding profusely and the other unconscious. Guided on the phone by ERCP Dr Santanu, essential pre-hospital care was administered and the two were rushed to the nearest hospital about ten kilometres away. Kumar ensured during the journey that all vitals were stabilized. In their heartfelt praise of the 108 team, the people of Padmabill have no hesitation in saying that without their help and care both the victims would have died.

Even as he showed us around the emergency response centre, Bhattacharya was on the telephone monitoring the response of his team to yet another tragic situation: the collapse of Secunderabad's iconic City Light restaurant.

When asked to compare 108 with the famous 911 of the USA, Bhattacharya said the Indian version's coverage is three times the total population of US with services in thirteen states and two union territories. And its coverage continues to grow as more states sign up. Also, adapting to Indian needs, it is expanding its response to include essential needs which are not a part of the 911 portfolio. Take for instance its contribution to reducing infant mortality rate, a critical Millennium Development Goal. Not only does it rush to the nearest hospital a woman already in labour, replacing, in difficult cases, a potentially dangerous home setting by institutional delivery, but two days later transports the proud mother back home with her baby in specially designed neo-natal care ambulances while giving her essential advice.

In another imaginative innovation, to deal with emergencies in flood-ravaged areas, they have developed boat ambulances. For inaccessible hilly areas, there are palkis!

The 108's response is not only to medical emergencies, but also to situations requiring urgent response by police or fire departments. In fact, to once again cite Bhattacharya, our lucid and articulate guide, the medical, police and fire emergencies often come as a single package! Indeed, in Hyderabad, so close is the collaboration with the police emergency response system that on 11 April 2013 (Ugadi Day) the then chief minister of undivided Andhra Pradesh, Kiran Kumar Reddy, inaugurated on the premises of GVK EMRI the Dial 100 Director General Command & Control Centre and dedicated it to the people of Andhra Pradesh. Till this day, the dial 100 was operational only in the district level. The calls used to land in the district police control rooms in which no PBX, software, voice logger etc. was present except for Hyderabad and Cyberabad. Today, all the 23 Districts of undivided Andhra Pradesh, 34 Police Control Rooms and 1600 police stations are connected to the DGCC centre through a common technology and telecom platform due to which real time information sharing and quick action can be initiated even in the remotest of the villages of Andhra Pradesh.

There is constant research-based upgradation of all facets of the service. Thus, for instance, emergency care skills have been further strengthened by collaboration with the Stanford University School of Medicine.

This service is entirely free. Inevitably, the overwhelming majority of beneficiaries are from economically weaker backgrounds. It is the kind of contribution for which it is difficult, if not meaningless, to assign a value in monetary terms.

Not surprisingly, 108 has become a household word even in remote villages with name recognition outstripping many well known brands.

A boat ambulance. Photo courtesy GVK EMRI

104: Health Information Helpline Services

A brief mention may be made here of Health Management and Research Institute (HMRI).

HMRI was launched as a non-profit organization working towards improved access and quality of healthcare services for all. Piramal Foundation is now its primary supporter. Though Tech Mahindra is not associated with its operations today, the original technology was incubated in Satyam Foundation of which Dr Balaji Utla, the current CEO of HMRI, was once the head. As he explained to us, it was based on the experience that many health issues can be resolved by just speaking to a doctor on the phone. 104 dial-in helpline services provide heath advice and information from qualified personnel for the sick and needy in remote areas. It leveraged state-of-the-art information and communication technologies and modern management practices to transform healthcare delivery to people in far flung areas.

Tech Mahindra takes great satisfaction in the fact that the technology initially developed by Satyam Foundation has enabled HMRI, through public-private not-for-profit partnerships to reach over 100 million beneficiaries belonging to vulnerable sections of the population in rural areas of several states in India.

To quote Praveen Raj Gullepalli of Tech Mahindra, 'Our public health IT platforms that are being used by EMRI 108 and the HMRI 104 are a standing testimony to the sterling efforts of the CSR wing of the Satyam-Mahindra Satyam-Tech Mahindra. They, more importantly, heralded the advent of "Thought Leadership" in corporate social responsibility efforts in India and the infusion of new, innovative thinking, unleashing the power of technology to make a substantial difference to the quality of life around us.'

17

Conclusion

As we look back at what the Tech Mahindra Foundation has achieved during its brief existence, we are filled with both pride and humility: pride at having been part of a venture that has transformed the lives of thousands of disadvantaged children and youth and humility at witnessing the vision, compassion and selfless service of many of our NGO partners. And few experiences have been more moving than the encounters with many young beneficiaries who have displayed amazing courage and determination in the face of most cruel and harsh odds.

TMF has always been very conscious of the fact that NGOs *on their own* do not have the capacity to meet all the development needs of the marginalized in our country; the state has the giant share of the resources and the matching responsibility. The more the two can work together, the better it would be for society. And so we have always encouraged our partners to ensure that the various government schemes designed for the poor reach those for whom they are intended. At the same time, we understand the reality that it is not always easy to work with the government. The obstacles the 'system' puts in the way of those seeking to solve the complex problems facing the poor in our inequitable society are well known. However, our own experience has been that there are many fine officials themselves struggling against corruption, lethargy and ubiquitous red-tape.

We have steered clear of the argument according to which NGOs, especially those funded by corporations as part of their CSR activities, working for the well-being of the underprivileged were giving the state an excuse to evade its responsibilities. I asked Anand Mahindra what he thought was the rationale behind

She has the right to a better future

supporting NGOs when providing education to all children was the responsibility of the state. To this, he had a pragmatic response: 'The problem is too vast, there is no single answer, no silver bullet. The government may provide free education. But there are many dimensions to the problem preventing a parent from sending a child to school. And even when the child does get to the government school, much supplementary help may be needed to ensure that the child gets proper education.' This logic, he felt, applied particularly to the girl child.

Tragically, it is in the field of education that India's performance has been truly dismal with the poor being the worst sufferers. Strategic analysts often compare India and China in military and economic terms. But one of the main reasons for the growing gap between the two is possibly in the quality of school education. The Programme for International Student Assessment (PISA) is a worldwide study by the Organisation for Economic Cooperation and Development (OECD) carried out in member and non-member nations. This study surveys the scholastic performance of 15-year-old school pupils in the areas of mathematics, science and reading. Of the 74 countries tested in the PISA 2009 cycle, two Indian states, Himachal Pradesh and Tamil Nadu selected for the test, came up 72nd and 73rd in both reading and maths, and 73rd and 74th in science. Shanghai students scored the highest in the world in every category (mathematics, reading and science). OECD described Shanghai as a pioneer of educational reform, noting that 'there has been a sea change in pedagogy'.

Amartya Sen's speech to the Commonwealth education conference, Edinburgh. October, 2003

'. . . HG Wells was not exaggerating when he said, in his Outline of History: "human history becomes more and more a race between education and catastrophe." If we continue to leave vast sections of the people of the world outside the orbit of education, we make the world not only less just, but also less secure.'

It is indeed the state's responsibility to fulfil its constitutional mandate of free and compulsory education for all children between six and fourteen years of age. It is the role of the voluntary sector to complement and supplement these efforts. An NGO with proper vision, commitment and skills identifies the areas where the state has failed. It reaches out to those marginalized children who, for a variety of complex reasons, are not getting quality education. This puts them at the risk of being perpetually trapped in a poverty cycle. For instance, a socially sensitive NGO develops a rapport with destitute communities which the state often fails to do. TMF made it its goal to seek out such NGOs which reach out to difficult-to-reach deprived children to provide them with quality education.

Since a major problem today is the quality of education being imparted in government run schools, an important contribution of the NGO sector is to rectify this problem. Many TMF partners have done outstanding work in this area. They devise pedagogies specially suited to the needs of disadvantaged children. These can serve as role models for government schools.

It is precisely TMF's concern about the quality of education in the municipal schools which has prompted it, under the leadership of its present CEO Loveleen Kacker, to enter into a partnership with the East Delhi Municipal Corporation (EDMC) to help set up an In-Service Teacher Education Institute (ITEI). To reinforce that experiment, in a three-way tie up, one of our star NGOs, Vidya and Child, has been invited to set up a lab school in the very school in which the ITEI is located.

In Chapter 5, I have spoken of another important recent initiative of TMF. Midway between government-run and purely private schools are 'government-aided' schools where the government involvement is limited to paying the teachers' salaries. Many of these schools are operating well below their potential largely because of the resource-crunch faced by the trusts running them. TMF has taken up the challenge to transform one of these schools under the very aptly named project: ARISE or All Round Improvement in School Education.

More than a decade ago, the PROBE Team in their 'Public Report on Basic Education in India' had demonstrated that, contrary to claims often made, an overwhelming majority of poor parents do wish to send their children to school. During our interviews, one slum-dwelling parent after another confirmed this. What is more, this extends almost as much to their daughters as to their sons. However, there is enough patriarchy in the tendency to send sons to fee-charging private schools, which they presume give better education, and daughters to free government schools.

Every now and then, a child 'drops out' prematurely from the educational system because of his or her family's economic circumstances. But that's just one side of the story. In fact, all too often, the child leaves because the parents perceive the quality of education to be of such low quality that they decide that it is better to have him/her work. One could say that, given the opportunity costs, it was a rational decision. And then there are children who have not dropped out but have been pushed out by the system by devices ranging from corporal punishment to caste-based discrimination, from imposition of hidden costs to absence of toilets for girls. The law, of course, will now endeavour to ensure that all children are enrolled. But we have still a long way to go before every child actually attends and, what is more important, acquires meaningful learning. In the meanwhile, good NGOs, like our partners, seek to bridge the gaps.

There is another far more complex challenge facing all of us involved in the educational sector. The six-year-old of today has to be prepared not for 2015 but 2025 or later! It is passé now to refer to the accelerating rate of technological change and the impact it is having on our lives. With a long-term vision and strategy, the NGO partners of TMF are taking care to give the children a broad-based foundation and ability to be lifelong learners. The need of the hour is to ensure that even children from impoverished backgrounds get sufficient grounding in science and technology. This, in fact, has been a continuous concern of TMF.

The challenge facing those running vocational training programmes is somewhat different. They have to ensure that their trainees get suitable placement as soon as possible after finishing the course. In fact, this was the criterion primarily used by us in judging a NGO partner working in this field. It was not always easy for us to assess the accuracy of the data provided by the NGOs, particularly in respect to whether the person held on to her/his job and even less so to their long-term career prospects. But, in most cases, our field executives were convinced that the trainees had acquired sufficient skills to be employable with reasonable salaries or, if they so preferred, to even be self-employed. While it was generally difficult to evaluate long-term impact, many of the skills imparted clearly have long shelf lives and built-in flexibility. It is to be hoped that the well-structured programme now being offered under Tech Mahindra SMART scheme will help in meeting this objective.

As we explained in Chapter X, Tech Mahindra SMART is now one of TMF's flagship programmes. To quote Loveleen Kacker:

'We are expecting to expand to 50 SMART centres by 2014–15 and to be able to train 10,000 youth annually and make them employable. Not only that, we also aim to set up 100 centres by 2016 and reach out to a larger pool of young men and women.

'In the next step, we would like to scale up the capacities of our existing centres to be able to reach out to 1 lakh youth, and also introduce SMART 2.

'With SMART 2, we intend to upgrade the skills of SMART beneficiaries who have been gainfully employed for some time and performing well in their jobs, but need to upgrade their skills to move on to the next stage of their career . . .'

We have been particularly fortunate in locating some excellent vocational training programmes for women. It was heartening to see slum-dwelling girls become confident para nurses; it was even more thrilling to see some of them become creative fashion designers. Then there is Katalyst, the amazing scholarship programme that enables bright girls from economically weak backgrounds to realize their dreams—even if the dream is to become an astrophysicist at NASA!

When spelling out the principles and priorities of TMF, the board of directors was quite clear that it would be a secular body. However, in recognition of the special problems faced by the country's largest religious minority, it would pay special attention to programmes designed to ensure their progress.

Some of the programmes supported by TMF are specifically targeted at Muslim girls. However, quite often, even though an NGO is broadly working for the betterment of the poor in society, a large proportion of the beneficiaries are Muslims. This merely underlines the unfortunate fact that this minority community occupies a higher percentage among the economically underprivileged—certainly in the urban centres in which TMF works—than their proportion in the overall population.

Our work, over and over again, brought us face to face with the social realities highlighted in the Sachar Committee report. The educational backwardness of Muslims in India should be understood in the wider context of their overall socio-economic and political marginalization. But clearly and perceptibly—vindicated by statistics—the situation is improving. A great joy of our work has been the opportunity to see brave Muslim girls defying stereotypes. One also discovered that simply because a woman decided to adopt an orthodox dress code most certainly did not mean that she was a voiceless passive acceptor of irrational barriers. As Benazeer of Raza showed, irrespective of the clothes they choose to wear, these women can think boldly and plan a brave future for the next generation.

What is most encouraging is that there is a perceptible generational change. Mothers themselves may be illiterate but they are ensuring that their daughters go to school and then go on to follow vocations of their choice.

TMF's partners have not only empowered women but in many cases helped break conservative taboos, enabling girls to come out and rise to their true potential. But even more heartening is the courage of those parents—mostly mothers but also many fathers—who are willing to defy the peer pressures of getting their girls married young and, instead, encouraging them to forge ahead in pursuit of their dreams. Every parent—father or mother—I met was determined that daughters will not be forced into early marriage but will be allowed, indeed encouraged, to study as far as she likes or

Mothers and daughters combine to promise India a new future

has the potential for. Of course, one must allow for two caveats: the parents interviewed were precisely those whose children were being taught by our partner NGOs with progressive ideas and so were not strictly representative of the general population; secondly, the parent while speaking to me may have felt the need to articulate publicly 'politically correct' sentiments, not necessarily reflecting their actual future behaviour. Having said that, so widespread was the sentiment against early marriage and in favour of maximum possible education of the girl and so spontaneous the assertions, one is inclined to believe at least in metropolitan India, that social revolution is taking place to which TMF has made a small contribution.

Sociology students have waiting for them dozens of exciting research projects about urban social dynamics. In one poor illiterate family after another, the next generation is getting educated and venturing out to professions and perspectives undreamt of by their parents.

To truly appreciate the significance of the work being done by our NGO partners, one has to consider the kinds of challenges that are deeply embedded in social work. Take, for instance, the education of a child from an economically weak family. The child was perhaps malnourished from birth with inevitable impact on her cognitive growth. She may reside in a dingy single room *jhuggi*, traumatized by an alcoholic father abusing her mother. She is with the teacher for a maximum of five hours and then returns to the same problem-plagued environment. Neither of her probably illiterate—or near-illiterate—parents may be of much help in her homework; the noise of the neighbours squabbling at the water tap is likely to shatter any sort of peace that might help her concentrate on work. If, in the midst of all this, an NGO is able to get the child to secure even barely pass marks it has done a remarkable job. Of course, there was no dearth of cases where a bright child from this background was helped by the NGO to rise to an astonishing level.

Our work with the NGOs empowering the physically challenged has been a source of continuous learning. EnAble India's founder, Shanti Raghavan, who has, for more than a decade, been preparing persons with disability (PWD) for the jobs that they eventually take up, offers a perceptive perspective on the issue. She feels companies do not realize that PWDs can be an alternate source of suitable employees, who can contribute to overall diversity, creativity and workplace morale, which can enhance their organization's image and productivity.

In many ways, the most exciting work done by the Foundation relates to the empowerment of the visually impaired. We have been specially privileged in having as our partners some of the most outstanding persons working in the field, many of them blind themselves. With profound understanding of the needs and possibilities in this area—including the newer avenues being opened up by technology—they have made most effective use of our grants. Their insightful domain knowledge and unfailing dedication greatly contributed to strengthening our work in this field. We were greatly enlightened by comments such as this one, from our partner George Abraham, himself visually impaired: 'Blindness is not the real problem, it is the way we think.' Over the brief period of its existence, the Foundation has diligently carved out a niche for itself in this field, culminating in the establishment of a network of our partners appropriately named Vision for India. This, hopefully, will generate synergy as they share their experiences and, where possible, collaborate in joint endeavours to meet the various needs in this sector.

What was most gratifying was the acknowledgment, by several of our partners who are doing excellent work that

TMF was responsible for coming to their aid when they were struggling—in some cases as mere beginners; in others, as organizations that had been functioning for a while but whose potential had not been recognized by enough funding agencies. The statements recorded in earlier chapters from organizations such as Shashwat, Score, Anandwan and Akanksha's LTL testify to this willingness of TMF to take a risk where we were convinced that a new or a struggling organization was going to do good work.

It is not surprising that many of our partners have been honoured by the state or others for their work. Four of our colleagues, Dipendra, George, Shaheen and Shanti, are Ashoka Fellows. Shanti has also received the National Award for Empowerment of Persons with Disabilities, 2010, and was chosen as one of Mahindra-cum Times Now's Amazing Indians. In 2012, Uma Tuli and Geeta Dharmarajan were conferred the Padma Shri. I have little doubt that many more will be similarly honoured in the years to come. More importantly, there will be many who will be doing equally outstanding work even though they may not figure in any list of awards.

Katherine Boo's bestselling book *Behind the Beautiful Forevers* offers a vivid description of life in a Mumbai slum. But while the misery and squalor she describes is, sadly, realistic, her account misses out on some of the truly inspirational individuals and stories which emerge from these most unlikely of settings. Happily, we encountered many such extraordinary people in the course of our work.

One of the most heartwarming things about talking to the children being educated by our NGOs is the very large number who speak of their determination, when they grow up, to do something for others who come from equally vulnerable backgrounds. Some of them will no doubt get distracted by other attractions when they actually become adults, but many will carry this sense of responsibility with them onto their later lives. Many of our beneficiaries, who have declared their aspiration in life as wanting to help the fellow underprivileged, seem to echo Gandhiji who as usual put it simply but beautifully, 'The best way to find yourself is to lose yourself in the service of others.'

Tech Mahindra Foundation is not in the business of giving alms. It seeks to empower the young, no matter how handicapped by circumstances, to achieve their dreams, to have a sense of fulfilment at having been able to rise to their potential. It is our endeavour to ensure that they can look forward to a life of dignity and honour, and to be responsible citizens, hopefully helping others in the vulnerable circumstances of which they themselves have such rich experience.

We did not specifically go out to look for programmes affecting Dalits. But clearly they constitute a very high percentage of the poor and, in the case of KKPKP in Pune, probably 100 per cent! In urban India, it is not always easy to distinguish the SCs/STs from the general population. Many have moved out of traditional professions. And we are not talking merely of the 'creamy layer'. However, the majority are still trapped in the cycle of poverty. Clearly, the work of many of our partners will ensure that the next generation is different, with education and skills harmonizing with changing socio-economic dynamics of the country. Some of the most oppressive elements of the pre-independence social mores are withering away. But there is still a long journey ahead. In a recent study titled 'The Untouchables', Oliver Mendelsohn, and Marika Vicziany (2000, Cambridge University Press) argue that more progress has been made post-independence in relation to the abatement of adverse discrimination than in reducing poverty.

The merger of Mahindra Satyam with Tech Mahindra and the growing profits of the company have led to a very substantial enhancement of the funds made available to the Foundation in recent years. This has enabled the Foundation to greatly enlarge its sphere of activities.

Many factors have contributed to the Foundation's success, among which one of the most important is the sensitivity of the leadership of the Tech Mahindra company to the problems faced by the economically, physically and socially underprivileged in the country. Vineet Nayyar has devoted much time and energy to the Foundation right from the outset. Then there is CP, who, when I asked him about his enthusiastic support to TMF, said: 'Disparities in our society stare us in the face. We must all do what we can to bridge the gap between the haves and the have-nots.'

My colleagues in the Foundation constantly astonished me with their commitment. And we could always rely on logistical assistance from the Tech Mahindra company as a whole.

Little help from the TMF has helped make many dreams come true. But success has many parents: the family with its faith in the potential and rights of their child, willing to challenge orthodoxy and stereotypes; then there is the inspirational 'didi' of the NGO who believes in the child and often becomes the role model for the child; but, above all, it is the child herself/himself . . . brave, determined, exuding optimism.

We at TMF do not wish to exaggerate our contribution. We are realistic about our limitations and those of our partners. The sheer magnitude and complexity of the problems facing our society compels humility. But there is no doubt that the country is on the move. And TMF, along with other members of the large, socially responsible Mahindra family—led by Keshub and Anand—is a committed and dedicated part of this vibrant phenomenon.

Acknowledgements

First of all, I am most grateful to our NGO partners. I had known practically all of them even before I began writing this book. As I travelled around the country, I was repeatedly overwhelmed by their humility, their passion, their skills.

I am deeply indebted to all the staff members of the Tech Mahindra Foundation who worked with me during the five years that I had the privilege of leading the team. Their youthful energy and dedication ensured that I rarely was reminded of the fact that I myself had entered my seventies. To these I would like to add the staff of the erstwhile Mahindra Satyam Foundation who came on board midway during this period. A word of thanks is also due to A.S. Murthy whose advice was of great help in ensuring a smooth merger.

A special mention must be made of Milind Kulkarni who, over and above his normal full-time duties in Tech Mahindra, performed multiple roles in support of the Foundation with unfailing cheerfulness and complete reliability. Many other associates of Tech Mahindra extended their support whenever we needed their help.

I would very much like to thank all the photographers whose work illustrates the book. Unfortunately, with the exception of Haran, Shaily and Sahil, who were engaged by me to cover some specific scenes in NCR, Bangalore, Mumbai and Pune, I do not have the names of many others whose photos were provided for the book by the various NGOs.

Like any other author I would like to acknowledge the hard work of all those in Penguin who, in one way or the other way, were involved in the production of this book, specially Ambar and Paloma.

I retired in March 2012 from TMF. I have tried to record also some of the most impressive work done later by the Foundation up to the end of 2013. I wish to thank my successor Loveleen Kacker and her team for the material relevant to this new period.

It was very kind of Anand Mahindra to contribute a thoughtful Preface.

A very special word of thanks goes to my friend Vineet Nayyar who has been the main inspiration behind the Foundation and on whose insistence this book was written.

I would like to conclude with a disclaimer. Except where I am explicitly quoting somebody, the views expressed in the book are mine and may not always be shared by Tech Mahindra or the Tech Mahindra Foundation.